The Essence
of Good Teaching

*Helping Students
Learn and Remember
What They Learn*

Stanford C. Ericksen

The Essence
of Good Teaching

 Jossey-Bass Publishers

San Francisco • London • 1988

THE ESSENCE OF GOOD TEACHING
Helping Students Learn and Remember What They Learn
by Stanford C. Ericksen

Copyright © 1984 by: Jossey-Bass Inc., Publishers
350 Sansome Street
San Francisco, California 94104
&
Jossey-Bass Limited
28 Banner Street
London EC1Y 8QE

Library of Congress Cataloging in Publication Data

Ericksen, Stanford C. (Stanford Clark) (date)
The essence of good teaching.

(The Jossey-Bass higher education series)
Bibliography: p. 167
Includes index.
1. College teaching. 2. Lecture method in teaching. 3. Education technology. 4. Motivation in education. 5. College students—Rating of.
I. Title. II. Series.
LB2331.E75   1984   378'.125   84-47983
ISBN 0-87589-615-4

Manufactured in the United States of America

The paper in this book meets the guidelines for permanence and durability of the Committee on Production Guidelines for Book Longevity of the Council on Library Resources.

JACKET DESIGN BY WILLI BAUM

FIRST EDITION
First printing: November 1984
Second printing: May 1985
Third printing: October 1987
Fourth printing: November 1988

Code 8436

The Jossey-Bass
Higher Education Series

Consulting Editor
Teaching and Learning

Kenneth E. Eble
University of Utah

To Jane,
who confirmed the dignity and value
of the individual and who insisted
that this book be written.

Preface

Teaching is the primary mission of a college, and whatever else might be said or done by way of educational reform, how well we—the teachers—do our job is absolutely basic. The demands on instruction change as society modifies and expands what it expects from higher education, as new resources for teaching become available, and as the criteria for evaluating the quality of instruction are sharpened. There is no consensus model of the ideal teacher, and the instructional diversity we see on every campus is a clear reminder that the individual teacher is the cook in charge of the kitchen. Each, however, will benefit from knowing more about the principles of pedagogical nutrition, that is, from understanding the underlying *constancies* required for good teaching. My purpose in writing this book, therefore, is to give the teacher a conceptual base for making decisions about how to do a better job in managing the classroom hour. More specifically, I hold that the payoff for good teaching is in terms of what students learn and carry away, and most of us strive to achieve this objective.

Good teachers skillfully cope with the *specific* demands of instruction, but they also possess a *fund of knowledge* about what they are doing. Successful professional practitioners generally score well on these two counts—they exercise specific skills for meeting particular problems, and they also understand why things work the way they do. Successful teaching is no different, and so my emphasis is on the conceptual underpinnings of good instruction.

My treatment of college teaching reflects lessons learned from being a long-time professor but especially from my twenty years at the Center for Research on Learning and Teaching at the University of Michigan. The roots of my position should be set forth: In 1962 a faculty committee recommended that a Center on Teaching be established, and its prospectus made clear that the success of this new unit would require that it offer something more than tinkering with "innovative" teaching. As the director, my first official action was to change the name to the Center for *Research on Learning and* Teaching. I had confidence that my discipline specialty—research on human learning and thinking—had reached a level of maturity that would allow useful extensions into the college classroom. From the beginning, therefore, my own perceptions of instruction have been selectively tilted toward how these findings on learning, memory, thinking (problem solving), motivation, and attitude change can be transformed to support college teaching.

These interpretations are the basis for this book. Chapter One sets the theme: The lasting measure of good teaching is what the individual student learns and carries away. The one piece of artwork in this chapter shows the outcome when teachers make full use of the intellectual and motivational resources students bring to the classroom. Chapter Two examines course content and shows how decisions on what to include reflect the teacher's understanding of the long-lasting relevance of selected units of knowledge. Most courses are composed of a combination of facts, skills, concepts, methods, and values, to which must be added the inevitable personal development of the individual student.

The next four chapters consider the instructional means

for tapping and releasing the resources for learning and remembering. The lecture is the usual mode for presenting information, and Chapter Three reviews this familiar form of teaching, as well as the teacher's role in making effective use of various technological aids—audiovisual devices, computers, and the printed word. Special attention is given to the importance of probing value implications, since this function will outlive a technology that places the organized world of knowledge literally at the fingertips of students. Motivation (Chapter Four) to learn is part of every teacher's responsibility and is best accomplished by the spontaneous display of interests, positive attitudes, and enduring values, which are signs to students about what is worth learning and retaining in their own store of knowledge. I hold that the reinforcing effects of satisfying curiosity are educationally more powerful than extrinsic rewards of test scores, high grades, or even honors. Meaning—comprehension or understanding (Chapter Five)—is the strongest single factor leading to long-term retention. Rehearsal, that is, active participation and review, is basic and thus the major focus of this chapter. Forgetting, however, is inevitable, and guides are given as to how the teacher can help reduce the influence of factors leading to forgetting; for example, discussion groups serve as an excellent means to gain retention through better understanding. The shift from memorizing specifics to comprehending concepts (Chapter Six) is an important step forward in college-level instruction. Understanding ideas is the target of teaching, because ideas with deep meaning endure over time and extend into different settings. Various instructional arrangements directly related to concept learning are briefly summarized, but in any given instance, each student shapes the fluid meaning of an idea against a distinctive and idiosyncratic personal store of knowledge.

Learning how to learn and to solve problems—thinking independently—is the most important single end product of education. Chapter Seven demonstrates that a teacher meets this special challenge best by staying within the boundaries of a particular discipline. Chapter Eight recognizes that it is hard for students to think straight if their emotions are in turmoil. Nearly all students will, sooner or later, feel the need to seek advice and coun-sel from a teacher whose judgment they trust. The empathetic teacher, as counselor or mentor, is especially helpful to those in need of remedial support in matters of study and learning.

Evaluative judgments (Chapters Nine and Ten) are intrin-sic to the academic enterprise and cannot be farmed out. The results of evaluation make a difference in the career progress of both students and teachers and therefore require considerable technical assistance to assure that procedures are valid. Quizzes have an important diagnostic and instructional function, and student ratings of a teacher offer significant data as a basis for self-improvement; in short, evaluations influence what and how well students learn and how well teachers do their job.

Chapter Eleven is teacher-oriented and identifies the sup-port teachers receive (or should receive) from their institutions for improving the quality of instruction. For one thing, the dis-tinctive strength of the individual teacher must be sustained—and by means other than exhortation or neglect. Providing in-formation based on sound research and effective practices at other institutions is a primary contribution to be made by a center on teaching. Chapter Twelve concludes the book with a perspective about the diet for the self-sustaining professor. Self-esteem is basic and is nurtured from sources beyond salary in-creases and promotion.

I have drawn freely from the *Memo to the Faculty* series, which I wrote or edited at the Center for Research on Learning and Teaching at the University of Michigan. These seventy-one newsletter-type analyses covered and re-covered many topics directly related to college teaching, and this book is essentially an integration and extension of the various themes first stated in the *Memos*. I have tried to use language appro-priate for the faculty as a whole, and this means, among other things, that I have had to be rather sparse in my use of illustra-tive examples taken from any one department.

The epigraphs for each chapter are a mixture of state-ments from classic writers and contemporary college teachers; they are offered as stimulating observations related to the substance within the chapters.

Having been a college teacher for more than forty years, I find it difficult to credit the source of ideas expressed in the pages that follow. I acknowledge my debt to my associates at the Center for Research on Learning and Teaching and my colleagues on the Panel on Research and Development of Instructional Resources within the Committee on Institutional Cooperation of the Big Ten universities. My peers in the Department of Psychology at Ann Arbor have consistently supported and encouraged my efforts to filter out the instructional implications from the findings of our discipline.

These have been exciting and rewarding years, and I treasure the memories of my work with students and my fellowship with teachers. For the past twenty-two years, my professional specialty has been to transform basic research and theory in psychology into support of college teachers. At times, professors can indeed be difficult, but I doubt if anyone has more respect and affection for college teachers than do I. For many years they have been the source for raising (and lowering) my self-esteem. They are a marvelous group of intelligent people who examine the meaning of accumulated knowledge and implement a set of enduring values for the benefit of the next generation of citizens. In the service of a democratic society, the contribution that teachers make stands alone at the top of the line.

Ann Arbor, Michigan   Stanford C. Ericksen
August 1984

Contents

The Author

Stanford C. Ericksen is professor emeritus of psychology at the University of Michigan. In 1962 he was the founding director of that institution's Center for Research on Learning and Teaching. He joined the Michigan faculty after fourteen years of being head of the Department of Psychology at Vanderbilt University. His A.B. degree (1933) and M.A. degree (1934) were from the University of Utah and his Ph.D. degree (1938) from the University of Chicago; all three degrees were in psychology.

      Ericksen's career-long research interest is in human learning and thinking and, for the past quarter century, in using these findings to support college teaching. His twenty-year *Memo to the Faculty* series reflects this purpose, as do such other publications as *Development and Experiment in College Teaching* (an annual, 1964–1981, compilation of instructional activities in the Big Ten universities), *Instruction: Some Contemporary Viewpoints* (with others, 1967), *Effective College Teaching* (with others, 1970), *Motivation for Learning: A Guide for the Teacher of the Young Adult* (1974), and *Support for Teaching at Major Universities* (1979).

Ericksen was director of National Project III (Fund for the Improvement of Postsecondary Education) and wrote or edited its sequence of eight reports: *Criteria—For the Evaluation, Support, and Recognition of College Teachers* (1975–1978).

The Essence
of Good Teaching

Helping Students
Learn and Remember
What They Learn

CHAPTER ONE

The Lasting Measure of Good Teaching

> Then let us not leave the meaning of education am-
> biguous or ill-defined. . . . For we are not speaking
> of education in this narrower sense, but of that
> other education in virtue from youth upwards,
> which makes a man eagerly pursue the ideal perfec-
> tion of citizenship, and teaches him how rightly to
> rule and to obey. . . . that other sort of training,
> which aims at the acquisition of wealth or bodily
> strength, or mere cleverness, apart from intelli-
> gence and justice, is mean and illiberal, and it is not
> worthy to be called education at all.
> —Plato, *The Laws*

By precept and example, good teachers give voice to knowledge
and beliefs linking the past to the present and to the future.
This prophetic touch requires knowing the subject matter and
having the courage to express judgments about values. Thus,
teachers, as do scholars and researchers, exercise the academic
traditions of open inquiry and exploration of the diversity of

values. An analysis of good teaching, therefore, involves considerably more than detailing the instructional techniques of telling things to students.

Many yardsticks are needed to measure competence because people observe different aspects of teaching in different settings and for different purposes. Further, all manner of instructional variations are called for by the nature of the subject matter, the characteristics of students, institutional expectations, and the teacher's own habits and predispositions. This chapter reviews some of the different ways teaching is judged, but gives emphasis to the kind of instruction designed to have a long-term impact on students. A leading educational researcher (Bloom, 1982, pp. 12-13) reflected a similar emphasis as he projected the future of his specialty: "My wish is for us to reduce our efforts devoted to predicting and classifying humans and for us to make more central in our research the variables, processes, and concepts that can make a vast difference in the teaching and learning of students. While much has already been done, these ideas are still at a very primitive stage."

The Many Measures of Teaching

Nearly everyone holds opinions about what is or is not "good" teaching and, given this reality, criterion standards that ensure fair play—to the institution, the teacher, and the students—are difficult to come by. In any instance, measurement requires a reference standard for defining a scale of judgments about "good," "better," or "best." Group results of student ratings of teachers, for example, are usually reported against statistical norms, but assessments by peers and administrators are interpreted against qualitative reference points that may or may not be useful as guides for improving specific skills of teaching.

Remote Measures of Teaching. Institutional language about teaching is usually couched in global terms. Janet Lawrence (1982) made this clear in her content analysis of the citations and the supporting documents offered by administrators, faculty, and students about nominees for one of the more prestigious teaching awards at a large university. She concluded, "If one created a composite of the outstanding teacher from the attributes mentioned most often, he or she would be an inspiring instructor who is concerned about students, an active scholar who is respected by discipline peers, and an efficient, organized professional, who is accessible to students and colleagues" (p. 9). Her analysis confirms that these award winners (over a thirteen-year span) were indeed outstanding individuals, but on the basis of the descriptive attributes used, we can only infer what these teachers did to have a long-term impact on students.

Relative (comparison) ratings about the overall competence of individual teachers may serve administrative purposes, but such ratings are vague about instructional particulars. The ambiguity about specific factors is illustrated by the assessment teachers make of themselves. "An amazing 94 percent rate themselves as above-average teachers, and 68 percent rank themselves in the top quarter in teaching performance" (Cross, 1977, p. 10). Where is the average point for good teaching?

In the search for a conceptual standard, reference is frequently made to teaching "models." Categorizing styles of teaching, however, does not take us far, since they usually exalt the stimulus side of teaching rather than identify what the teacher does to influence what students learn and remember. Finer discriminations often stop with the classifying process itself, but describing a model is only the front part, the persona, behind which lie the more subtle but specific effects of teaching that accumulate day by day. Except as a conversation piece about certain general characteristics of teachers, the concept of models is static and simplistic. Mannequins are models, but good teachers do not stand still. The subtitle, "No One Way," of Sheffield's (1974) excellent compilation of essays by twenty-three outstanding teachers in Canadian universities confirms the intrinsic diversity of college instruction.

One common stereotype about good teachers is that they are charismatic spellbinders who arouse listeners. Such a motivating influence is, of course, excellent insofar as it generates enthusiasm for worthwhile subject matter and is not just an ego trip on the part of the teacher. Proclaiming the teacher-as-artist produces self-enhancing arguments freeing teachers from the more stringent criteria of what happens to students. These are the teachers who are likely to say, "I did a good job of teaching today; whether or not my students learned anything is up to them." This self-serving position is a neat bypass of accountability for what happens to students and sets aside, forthwith, any responsibility for making use of contributions from the science of learning. A similar defensive stance is expressed here: "My job is to give my students an opportunity to observe the scholarly mind at work." Instruction by example is important, but it is not the whole of teaching.

At the other extreme are the mental disciplinarians, those teachers who hold that hard study will steel mind and character for the coming tests of strength after graduation. The goal of this classic theory of education is to exercise the muscles of the mind: the mental faculties of memory, reasoning, imagination, concentration, and moral judgment. Generations of students have been coerced into memorizing and executing precise procedures in the belief that the mental discipline involved was more important than the intrinsic value of what was being learned. Would that the educational process were so uncomplicated. It is precarious to hold that the *process* of memorizing and mental drilling benefits students above and beyond the *substance* of what is being learned.

The Teaching-Learning Connection. Not many will argue the point that, in the final analysis, the quality of teaching must be defined in terms of what happens to students. Measures of teaching are oversimplified if they limit attention to the stimulus side—how the teacher presents information. The trouble is that it is so much more convenient to observe and evaluate a teacher's *performance* than to assess the lasting reactions on each student. In a comprehensive research report, Hyman, Wright, and Reed (1975) noted the procedural pitfalls in assessing the long-term effects of schooling, but they were able, nonetheless, to detail the important conditions about how knowledge is retained and learning sustained. Fortunately, accumulated wisdom about college teaching confirms that certain things that teachers do make a significant difference in their long-term impact on students. We need more words for teaching, words that provide sharper discriminations about how the teacher influences motivation and values, learning, memory, problem solving, and learning how to learn and to think independently. The basic theme of this book is to underscore such actions.

Experienced teachers are aware of conflicting criteria of competence, the difference, for example, between one's public reputation and the private assessment of the quality of the work being done. Career success—salary increases and promotion—requires that the teacher give due regard to the totems and taboos about instruction held by the home institution. At the same time, career satisfaction is sustained by confidence in knowing that a good job is being done in terms of one's own standards. In this personal domain, good teachers select and organize worthwhile course material, lead students to encode and integrate this information in memorable form, ensure competence in the procedures and methods of a discipline, sustain intellectual curiosity, and promote learning how to learn independently. Attitudes are sharpened, values explored, and aspirations clarified. The list goes on, but always toward the constructive goal of enhancing what students will come to understand and carry away.

The diversity of college teaching precludes firm, prescriptive rules about how to do it; each teacher starts the term knowing that instructional adjustments will need to be made each day in developing the succession of topics. Fortunately, students adapt to and accept a wide range of teaching styles once they come to understand the idiosyncratic combination of traits and habits that compose the instructor's consistent self.

It may seem picky, but evaluating the teacher as a person is not the same as evaluating teaching as an interactive process. Institutional standards about teachers develop as a composite of what many different faculty members are like rather than as differentiating statements about what these people actually do in promoting the interchange between students and a body of knowledge. A valid appraisal of teaching must be anchored to what happens to the individual student because, in essence, *teaching is the interaction between two persons*: the instructor and the learner, the master and the apprentice.

Grouping students into classes does not significantly change what goes on inside the individual, the way motivation affects learning, or the process of learning. Students sitting side by side differ in their reactions to what the teacher says and does, and these individual differences must be taken into account in an accurate assessment of teaching. The importance of this analytical attention to the student as learner is confirmed when we listen to former students talk about how their opinions about a teacher changed from the first day of class to the last and over the following years. One person might recall the entertaining characteristics of a particular teacher or say of another, "At the time, I resented the heavy pressure this guy laid on us, but now I see he made a real difference in how I think [cognition] and what I believe [motivation]."

The Measure of Meaning, Memory, and Motivation

In my view, the moment of instructional truth occurs when a student grasps the meaning of an important idea; all else is means to the end of understanding. By precept and example, good teachers make use of the intellectual and motivational resources of students for learning the meaning of worthwhile ideas. Research on human learning, observations by experienced teachers, and reports from students combine to support the concept represented by the schematic diagram, Figure 1—an anchoring reference for much that follows in this book.

Figure 1 compares two kinds of learning—rote and meaningful—and shows their extension beyond the time of the final examination. Note the high retention of meaningful material—words, phrases, sentences—in contrast to the low level of recall of material learned by rote memory—numbers, nonsense syllables. The implications for teaching are clear: to replace intensive coverage of factual material in the interest of helping students to comprehend a fewer number of significant ideas—concepts, generalizations, themes, laws, procedural principles, discipline-linked values, and the like. These larger abstractions tie together otherwise isolated and specific pieces of information. Forgetting is countered because, as study proceeds, conceptual

Figure 1. Retention Contrast of Meaningful and Rote Materials.

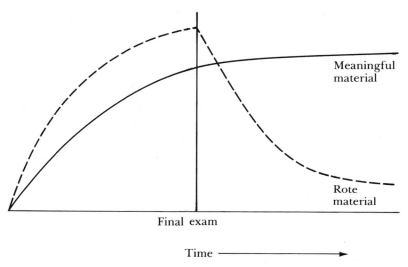

Meaningful material

Rote material

Final exam

Time ⟶

units become better organized and assimilated into the store of knowledge already in memory. This is the way the mind works, and we note such effects with everyday observations like, "The longer I live, the more convinced I am that [a particular idea or belief] is true."

How does this educational bonus come about? The answer is in terms of the constructive and cumulative effect of rehearsal (review and active participation). Almost any material can be remembered if it is practiced enough—for example, writing one's signature or driving a car. If some items of information seem less long lasting, it is usually because they receive less practice—for example, some parts of the multiplication table, telephone numbers, ZIP codes, and which U.S. vice-presidents served which presidents. The process of learning is one of active engagement by way of elaborating, integrating, organizing, coalescing, and consolidating new material with what is already known—the transformation of shallow meaning into a deeper level of understanding. Thus, rehearsal is the key factor for retention (see Chapter Five).

Information gains utility as the gist of its meaning is confirmed by subsequent experience. The practical exigencies of raising children, for instance, amount to a rehearsal of the meaning of textbook concepts once studied in a formal course. The continued reading of novels verifies course-given criteria of literature. Watching and participating in the social scene confirm the validity of principles first examined in courses in economics, political science, and sociology. Seeing these ideas in action is a form of review that supports and extends the personal meaning of a student's repertoire of knowledge—the solid line increment in Figure 1. These carryover effects are enhanced by teachers who provide frequent examples of how a given concept or methodological principle is reinforced in later (advanced) courses or in settings away from the classroom. Such illustrations give students the opportunity to actually practice the extension of ideas from teachers and textbooks into varying contexts (Chapter Six).

Even so, there is resistance. For many students, the evidence of a "good" course is filling a notebook with facts, feeling overwhelmed with new information, and being able to answer lots of concrete questions. The straight lines and square corners of factual information are, however, quickly blurred; the rate of forgetting is disarming. Memorized minutiae and footnote data have little meaning, and it is difficult to keep these "answers" in mind over time.

The contrasting effects shown in Figure 1 apply generally and simply indicate that meaningful learning lasts longer; it is value received for the students' money and for their time and effort as learners. The graph is a meld of three requirements for good instruction that have been recognized by experienced teachers long before learning theory got into the act to add its support:

1.   The substantive information in the course must have carryover value—something worth knowing in its own right or because it leads to further learning and strengthening of beliefs. Neither the teacher nor the students can anticipate in detail the time and place for future retrieval, but the teacher is the better judge of what information will likely be

relevant in later courses and in the off-campus settings (Chapter Two).

2. Carryover information must be thoroughly learned—that is, rehearsed. In the mind of a student, the *depth* of meaning gained from learning has a strong controlling influence on the subsequent life history of an idea.

3. Motivation is the energy that keeps the mental wheels turning. The steady state of the solid line in Figure 1 is a joint function of understanding the meaning of words and symbols and believing that they are worth remembering. A system of values serves as a binder for the retention of facts, concepts, and procedures.

Playing to Strength. Memorizing is not the strong suit of teachers or students. What is? The preceding three attributes of good instruction play to the strength of both participants. Teachers are at home in the management of ideas, and the teacher's knowledge of a subject is the basis for identifying material likely to hold lasting relevance for students.

The most powerful intellectual force in academia is the ability to derive and to use abstract ideas. In Plato's *Republic,* philosophers were kings because they were the ones most capable of freeing themselves from the constraining environment of the sensory world. In this sense, philosophical thinking should flavor every course. Further, and in a literal sense, students can only think for themselves; thus, the effects of personal meaning prevail. Writing in the sixteenth century, Montaigne expressed the gist of individuality in student thinking with a delightful metaphor, "Bees here and there suck this and cull that flower, but afterwards they produce honey which is peculiarly their own, and is no longer thyme or marjoram."

The easy route for teaching is to emphasize the acquisition of factual knowledge, the display of specific skills, and the ability to repeat memorized information. Measurable products of this order often carry more instructional weight than they should. A more appropriate use of cognitive talent is to organize a course around an explicit set of concepts and methodological principles. The frequently expressed aim, "My job is to teach my students to think like a mathematician [or architect, political scientist, or biologist] thinks," is an intellectual challenge to teacher and students alike. It is a solid purpose but more easily said than done. The problem is to differentiate memorizing from thinking and then to measure success. A well-designed final examination is, at least, an interim measure of how well a student can manage the complexities of course-based concepts.

Substance and Style. These pages have little to say about the style and techniques of teaching. Every teacher has a style, and Eble (1980) makes the important point that "teaching style" is not a superficial but a consistent display of the real character and personal values of the teacher. All teachers can offer examples of their own former teachers who showed a pervasive identification with their discipline and its significance for the future of their students; such teachers seemed to like ideas more than teaching, were willing and able to project what knowledge was worth knowing, and used the intrinsic challenge to understand as the major motivating influence for students.

I remember well a master teacher—one who never won an institutional award for outstanding skill as a craftsman. He taught an undergraduate course in comparative neurology, and the scope of his knowledge seemed to have no limit as he talked about biology in general or about neurological specifics. His enthusiasm peaked, however, with the synaptic nervous system of the earthworm and what makes him-and-her such a distinctive event in the biological scale of things.

Contrived signs of affection were never given to us, but we sensed that he enjoyed our company. He did not have instructional flair or an engaging lecturing style; he mumbled, and we strained to hear him. His discourse was often blocked with "ah-ah-ah," and we helped him find the right word. His blackboard sketches needed, and received, corrections. Just the same, there was no apology in his conviction that amazing knowledge could be found in the one small section of the curricular cafeteria that he was serving. He was more than willing to help any student who was curious to know more about why the earthworm was a good place to begin to comprehend the biological basis of behavior. Professor Jones loaded us with factual information, but the data did not stand by themselves; they were linked to the complex conceptual arrangements needed to understand the development of the phylogenetic scale. Trying to be a prophet was probably the last thing on his mind, but he had this touch as he stressed the significance of what we were learning as it related to our further studies in zoology, medicine, or psychology (Ericksen, 1974).

The passage of time and technological inventions have not changed the human dimensions of teaching. Students will always benefit from "earthworm" professors whose impact derives from their enthusiastic commitment to the enduring value of the substance of their subject-matter specialty, their insistence that material be thoroughly learned, and their precept and example. When the last class hour is ended, good teachers have weakened, if not cut, the instructional dependencies of their students by leading them to exercise, independently, their continued pursuit of knowledge within a framework of values.

As this chapter notes, many *public* measures of teaching exist, but I emphasize the *private* measure held by the teacher working toward a long-term impact on students. This anchoring conception is represented by Figure 1, which shows the constructive effects of three measures for good teaching: (1) identifying knowledge as having enduring value, (2) leading students to gain thorough understanding of the meaning of this knowledge, and (3) generating and sustaining the motivation to learn and remember. The whole enterprise of teaching is managed in terms of the *substance* of a course of study, analyzed in the following chapter.

CHAPTER TWO

Decisions About Course Content

> As regards the choice of *material,* it is essential that
> from the outset the child be made acquainted only
> with the best that is available. This implies that the
> Master is competent to recognize the best in the
> mass of erudition open to him. . . .
> —Erasmus, *De Ratione Studii*

Students find ways to adapt to less-than-exciting styles of teaching, but compensatory mechanisms are not available for what should have been taught but was not. They listen in good faith to what their teachers have to say, and this trust in their teacher's decisions about course content must not be misplaced. Colleges and universities select their teachers in terms of demonstrated competence in a subject and help the faculty keep abreast of changing knowledge by means of sabbatical leaves and funds for travel, research, and professional development. Educational validity rests on the subject-matter expertise of the faculty, and the only instructional sin greater than teaching obsolete or trivial information is to test and grade students about such knowledge.

I call attention to course content early in this book because the first major component of good teaching is the quality of information presented to students—the substance of the material composing the Y-axis in Figure 1 in the preceding chapter. "The content of instruction is more important than its form. ... A decade of educational experimentation in the public schools and in military and industrial training indicates strongly that the most important results have not been produced by changes in instructional method, nor by use of computers or audiovisual devices, but rather by changes in instructional content" (Rothkopf, 1973, pp. 123-124). Decisions about course content and its organization are made prior to the first day of class and reflect the depth and breadth of a teacher's understanding about the long-lasting relevance of selected units of information. Despite the short-term appeal of an entertaining, charismatic lecturer, the long-term impact of a course depends on its substance. Abrami, Leventhal, and Perry (1982) found that while such a lecturer might elevate student ratings, the content of a lecture showed a greater effect on course achievement.

The curriculum is in a continuous state of flux; deleting, integrating, and extending course content is probably the most active dimension within instruction. Good teachers do not offer the same course twice; new information is introduced, goals are clarified, the reference list is revised, existing principles are modified by recent findings, links with surrounding disciplines are strengthened, and areas of application are extended. The changes from one year to the next may be small, but the cumulative effect keeps the curriculum up to date. The validity of decisions about what students are expected to learn is a fundamental measure of good teaching. It was not always so.

In a former day, the liberal arts college was a finishing school where children of the elite acquired the signs and signals of the ruling class and returned to take their places as "leaders" in society. They could recite lines of poetry, repeat Newton's laws, execute the binomial expansion, and identify Greek and Roman classics. Students were set to the task of memorizing knowledge, and the memorizing process, per se, was valued over the factual, conceptual, and methodological content of what was being learned. Mental discipline was presumed to account for the benefits of instruction students might take with them. Change comes slowly in higher education, and Herbert Spencer was overly optimistic in 1860 when he said, "The once universal practice of learning by rote is daily falling into discredit."

In the protest days of the 1960s, students were in a hurry to do something about society's problems; they spoke for greater curricular "relevance." The press for social pragmatism came as quite a shock to teachers unaccustomed to being questioned about the worth of course content. This period of unrest, however, was soon followed by the narcissistic "self-realization" overtones of the counterculture. Conflicting values are indigenous to campus life as guardians and critics of higher education continue to debate curricular ends and instructional means. In what ways, for example, might greater emphasis be given to science and mathematics, second-language learning, career preparation, basic study skills, remedial instruction, and the ambiguous but never-ending issues relating to the "quality of life"? All schools, departments, and individual teachers wrestle with value judgments about what knowledge will sustain the force of instruction.

Defining Course Objectives

Exposing students to the light of knowledge by covering the field—the sunburn theory of instruction—is inadequate as the aim of a course. It does not do justice to the finer discriminations a teacher can make about how to organize a complex body of information so that students understand and retain it. Preparing a clear statement of course objectives is a demanding task requiring the best talent, if not the prophetic power, of a teacher. Two questions are ever present: (1) At what time in the future will the significance of a given segment of knowledge pass its inflection point and start downhill toward obsolescence? (2) Is it stepping-stone information or something to be learned for its own long-term value?

Intellectual browsing and pedagogical serendipity have their place, but instruction organized around a sequence of objectives makes more efficient use of students' talents for learning and understanding. Vague general goals such as "to appreciate the rigors of experimental psychology," "to cherish the values of classic literature," or "to analyze the basic findings of organic chemistry" are almost impossible to assess, and they excuse the teacher from accountability. Students are left wondering exactly what they are expected to learn and understand.

The opposite extreme is equally unproductive: performance objectives require students to make particular responses, to answer certain kinds of questions, to solve specific sets of problems. Neither students nor teachers like to be mentally fenced in by such predefined templates. I recall a scene where an instructional technician was making the "performance objective" pitch to a group of physics professors. They became so irritated by the testing trivia called for that they came close to asking the speaker to shut up and sit down. A good course contains more than can be sampled by a machine-scorable examination.

Good instruction calls for consistency among the three basic aspects of teaching: defining course objectives, managing the classroom hour, and devising methods of testing and evaluation. Students will privately, and sometimes publicly, complain when teachers wander too often from the announced course objectives or if examination questions are far removed from what is talked about in class. The intimate connection between goals and grades is frequently overlooked. It is inconsistent, for example, to proclaim you are teaching students how to think, to solve problems, and to discriminate values but then to test achievement in terms of the ability to memorize. One acid test of the internal consistency between goals and testing is the linkage between pronouncements made the first day of class and the kinds of questions on the final examination. Consistency is a matter of fair play, and students should know from the beginning what standards are to be met by the end of the course.

Incidental Learning. The idiosyncratic interests of each student are not denied; incidental learning is a constancy of in-

struction. A teacher's statements about course goals may help
to establish a set toward these ends, but they do not erase the attention students give to items on the instructional periphery.
From the teacher's point of view, minds wander. In addition to
tracking the target topic defined by the teacher, each student
picks up and encodes incidental information. Most of this is
quickly forgotten, but some becomes integrated into the student's long-term memory to influence further learning and
thinking. Incidental learning reflects the motivational and intellectual individuality of each student for composing the final
educational package that is carried away when the course ends.
The emphasis by the teacher on the primary goals of the course
must not, however, be compromised, because these goals anchor
the inevitable side trips by the individual students.

What voice should students have in this matter of defining primary course objectives? In a formal sense, not much,
since students do not know the subject as well as their teachers
do. The teacher's greater perspective about the technical aspects of the course material and the integrating concepts leads to
judgment about information and skills likely to carry over to
other courses and to jobs and experiences later. Students certainly know what they care about, and these interests guide
their direction and attention toward subsets of personal goals
within the context of the formal course.

One widely practiced arrangement for adapting to individual students is to negotiate a contract between student and
teacher. The teacher marks out the boundaries of the subject
and is explicit about the major areas, concepts, skills, and topics
for which competence is expected. The teacher generally controls the primary resources—texts, references, and lectures—
from which students derive their information. Within these limits, the opting student is responsible for formulating a particular
set of personal objectives that tap his or her own motivation
and talents for learning. The range of these variations will be
less in a tightly bound technical course than in a free-ranging
seminar or in independent study. Different students may contract to review so many books, to reach certain score levels on
tests, to write one or more papers, to execute a special project,

and so forth. These are stated as quantities, but the teacher must make the final judgment about the quality of the end product. This assessment of standards of quality cannot be compromised.

Standards of Mastery. In the absence of statements about standards of mastery, the goals of learning have not really been set. Learning at the level of simply recognizing that a proposition is true or false is quite a different standard from being able to retrieve a principle from memory to solve an otherwise novel problem. An impressive statement about course aims is of no avail if the evaluation of student achievement is tangential to the purpose of in-depth comprehension. The importance of *mastery* learning should be emphasized. This concept means that, rather than sampling how much has been learned during a given period of instructional exposure, study continues until a satisfactory level of competence has been achieved—as defined by the teacher. Given the time restraints of the academic schedule, the goal of mastery is often compromised—at least for the slower students—but it is a standard worth working toward. For one thing, the educational experience of achieving mastery is in itself a strong stimulus for students to sustain their study efforts.

The counterpart of these two options, mastery or partial learning, has a long history in the research analysis of learning: In one condition, the experimental subjects work until a preset level of performance (mastery) is achieved, or they are given a certain number of *trials* or time to demonstrate how much they have learned. In the instructional setting, the criterion of trials (partial learning) usually prevails because the academic term allows only a given number of lectures, laboratory periods, or discussion sessions before the curtain comes down and grades are turned in. In principle, however, the performance criterion of mastery should prevail for the primary objectives of a course. If comprehension is shallow, retention will be shallow.

The lockstep system of education was not invented by teachers interested in guarding the mastery criterion of learning. The pressures within the mass educational system favor instruction for learners who achieve mastery on time. Certainly, noncredit courses in the remediation or developmental category should be set up along mastery lines. These students should not move into the mainstream until they have demonstrated competence in the basic skills and information required for success in the usual college course.

A General Taxonomy for Course Content

This section examines some common cognitive categories for processing information that cut across instructional lines between departments: facts, performance skills, concepts, methods, and values. The substantive content in most college courses can be placed within this taxonomic array. Each of these categories has certain distinctive teaching-learning features that should be taken into account in arranging the sequence of topics and their manner of treatment. The following analysis is based on findings from research on human learning and memory, but each teacher must make the necessary adaptations to fit the conditions of a particular course.

Factual Information. Factual information is important in its own right and as a base for understanding higher-order principles. It is sometimes difficult, however, for students to grasp the kind of meaning essential for storing the message in long-term memory. The rote learning of facts is not usually as intrinsically interesting as is acquiring a new skill or comprehending and testing the meaning of a larger principle. Consequently, students depend on support and guidance from the teacher to master the meaning of factual data, that is, for integrating facts within a conceptual frame of reference. As is echoed throughout this book, understanding what something means is the strongest countervailing force to the steep curve of forgetting.

A particular point about memorization needs mention here because some degree of memorizing is usually involved when facts are linked to a body of information already in memory. This integration occurs via all manner of mnemonic schemes: elaborating the factual specifics into a meaningful story or rhyme or finding what, to the learner, are key words (Bellezza, 1982). The ancient method of *loci* may also be helpful: pairing a sequence of facts with specific points in a familiar physical location—a route across campus or the traffic pattern in one's home. Visual imagery is, for many, an important supplement to the semantic (verbal) schemes used for learning and retention. The value of mnemonic arrangements for rote learning has been well established, although these arrangements do, at times, seem rather gimmicky. There is no substitute for establishing a broad base of meaning for factual information, to place the specific data within the frame of reference of a larger set of ideas, concepts, principles, and themes.

Thus, in addition to helping students arrange some kind of mnemonic pegboard, effective teaching of factual material involves the figure-ground relationship—placing the facts within a larger context. Talking about when and where and who signed what peace pact is, for example, quite a different matter from developing an understanding of what this treaty means. The factual data are presented within the conceptual context, the theory, methods, and values that give meaning within a discipline to the factual body of knowledge. Teachers appreciate the importance of particular facts; students should hear why teachers have that appreciation so students can develop their own understanding of such information. The isolated presentation of facts is done well by books, computers, and other media, and the special emphasis by the human teacher is to develop and illustrate those ideas, methods, and values that give meaning to the particulars. The encoding process used by the individual student will not be exactly the same as the teacher's, but a model has to be set in regard to the significance of factual information.

Performance Skills. Dental education is a good example of the close interchange between performance skill and intellectual understanding. While we sit and squirm in a dentist's chair, we appreciate evidence of manual dexterity but we also have confidence that the dentist knows why a particular procedure is best. In most areas of instruction involving performance skills— art, dancing, music, graphics, medicine, nursing, and physical therapy, for example—the actual execution of a skilled act expresses, at the same time, the performer's mental schema of what to do and the sequence of action. The concentration of musicians, dancers, and athletes is a form of mental guidance for the fast-moving chain of responses. With practice, control of movement is extended to lower centers but judgmental decisions are not forsaken. Rehearsal, in one form or another, contributes to both performance and comprehension. As a matter of fact, the observed improvement as the performer practices and practices and practices is the visible counterpart of parallel cognitive rehearsal. The criticism of academic credit for "muscle twitching" does not apply to the process of learning a skill but only to the value of the end product, for example, basket weaving.

Forming Concepts. The flow of ideas dominates most college courses for two good reasons: (1) ideas cover more ground than do memorized specifics and (2) they tap the distinctive talents of students. Ideas take many forms: concepts, beliefs, principles, generalizations, hypotheses, theories, convictions, and images. By whatever label, the central ideas in a course serve as nodal points for the hierarchical arrangements of the supporting data, the logical arguments, and the value systems that pervade the course. Understanding concepts is important in its own right in addition to being a critical base for problem solving. Glaser (1984, pp. 98-99) made this clear: "Our research suggests that the knowledge of novices is organized around the literal objects explicitly given in a problem statement. Experts' knowledge, on the other hand, is organized around principles and abstractions that subsume these objects." This view is confirmed by Larkin, Heller, and Greeno (1980, p. 56): "The completeness of the problem representation clearly depends on the amount and organization of the problem solver's knowledge of concepts and principles. This complex interrelationship between knowledge of concepts and principles and knowledge of problem-solving procedures has been a central concern of current problem-solving studies." Since concept teaching is so basic, all of Chapter Six is given to this topic.

Methods of Analysis. A pedagogical invention for teaching students to be efficient problem solvers would truly be front-page news—but don't wait for it. This unrealized educational goal has been with us for a long time, and most teachers are willing to settle for teaching the analytical tools within a restricted domain of their discipline. Humility is in order because it is easier to teach facts, skills, and concepts than methods of inquiry and the procedures for solving problems. Greeno (1983, p. 80) interprets the current state of research and theory to mean that "analyses of the structure of information in a discipline . . . are not sufficient for instruction, because they do not include aspects of knowledge required for solving problems and for reasoning."

Instruction about methodology in an introductory course should be delayed because it is difficult for students to appreciate an early treatment on procedures while they are still wondering about the specific content in the field they have set out to study. When matters of methods and procedures are engaged, it is helpful for the teacher to identify specific labels, names, or symbols as handles for talking about these things and as preparation for their application as students carry out special projects, do lab work, complete homework assignments, make field observations, solve sets of assigned problems, and abstract pertinent literature. Teaching the problem-solving (research) methods of a discipline—for example, a statistical procedure, calibration of laboratory instruments, and bibliographical searching—is a two-level instructional task. The actual procedures may be concrete and specific, but the rationale for their use is likely to be an array of abstract principles—a demanding challenge for a teacher.

Changing Values. I now break the chain of taxonomic categories tied to the substantive content of a course by shifting attention from the facts, skills, and concepts students learn to the reshaping of attitudes and values. Teachers influence the interests, feelings, and beliefs of students and, at times, their aspirations and ambitions. These affective components of personal growth and development intermingle with the intellectual. A student's self-concept matures as feelings of competence and mastery emerge from understanding the substance of a course and its value implications. Without necessarily intending to do so, teachers model how the values of a specialist on a subject interact with one's personal beliefs as a citizen and as a member of the academic community.

Some teachers get carried away by the lures of the affective interchange and move outside the subject-matter track as they strain to be liked by students. They become educationally permissive, engage in intellectual wanderings, and distribute emotional palliatives designed to keep students happy—but uninformed. This fixation on affective tangentials shortchanges the cognitive goals of instruction and the related motivation.

Changes in interests, attitudes, and values are inevitable, and it is redundant to write "personal development" as a formal goal for a course. It is, however, appropriate for the instructor, on the first day of class, to talk about the attitudes and values that will be expressed during the course and to mention that the students might expect some reshaping of values to occur. Putting these matters squarely on the table forestalls possible charges of thought control, indoctrination, or propaganda. Perceptive students respond to these honest and forthright expressions positively or negatively; they rarely remain neutral. They realize that a great deal more is carried from a course than what is sampled on the final examination. Sharpened attitudes, deepened values, changing interests, new curiosities, redirected enthusiasms, and clarified aspirations are only part of the list of changes in the personal development of students actively engaged in a course of study.

Crossing Departmental Barriers

In a large university, individual members of a department are expected to guard the turf marked by boundaries set many years ago. When carried to an extreme, such intellectual provincialism becomes narrowly self-serving—a form of academic nationalism. Reordering curricular materials in a cross-disciplinary manner is good evidence that the participating teachers are concerned about keeping the substance of education in line with the kinds of problems students will meet in a changing social world. Unfortunately, prevailing mechanisms of recognition and reward in disciplines and institutions encourage many teachers to stand conservatively behind the traditional values of a departmental culture; interdisciplinary courses have a hard time getting started and surviving. It takes courage to be an advocate for "new" ways to serve the educational interests of students; it also takes depth and breadth of knowledge.

Interdisciplinary Offerings. The particular advantage of a cross-disciplinary course is the integration of data, methods, and theories of two or more fields to understand a theme or problem that generated the new offering in the first place. Simply exposing students to a seafood platter of different points of view is too casual; it does not reflect the intellectual maturity necessary to reevaluate and reinterpret a familiar body of knowledge in the light of findings from neighboring fields of study. An undergraduate seminar on, for example, Food, Fire, and Freedom (the interlock among global economy, energy, and human rights) would test the validity of ideas from several social sciences. A single teacher could handle some of these complexities, but a cooperative venture among specialists would enhance the cohesive theme.

Most of the major problems of the world today, and for the foreseeable future, call for the integrated contribution of different sets of data. Interdisciplinary offerings may not have strong buffering protection by a given department, but this does not detract from the educational merit of bringing about a refreshing and updated interchange among teachers from fields related to the new task at hand. Some of these recombinations disappear with the waning enthusiasm of their proponents, but others merge into the standard fare of a department or mark the beginning of a new academic unit. An interdisciplinary offering is a pilot program for keeping the curriculum relevant for students planning ahead.

In-the-Field Experiences. A related curricular development results from the stepped-up traffic on the two-way street between campus and community. Properly used, the off-campus setting is an excellent means for breaching ivy-covered walls (Sherman, 1982). It offers teachers more instructional elbow-room than is given by the square classroom in which students sit on bolted-down seats with the teacher up front talking about bolted-down ideas. In-the-field supervision allows students to sample the demands and rewards of potential career alternatives and to appraise otherwise unknown aspects of life in the community: in hospitals, mental health clinics, prisons, preschools, senior citizen centers, political campaigns, government agencies, business enterprises, and unions. Off the campus, students receive a tempered version of the school of hard knocks, and even a brief apprenticeship promotes structure and meaning to otherwise abstract conceptions about problems in today's communities and how some people spend their working lives.

These outreach arrangements go by different names: experiential learning, community service programs, cooperative education, and work-study arrangements, for example. Faculty members participate as sponsors, coordinators, consultants, advisers, and, occasionally, as teachers. Insofar as credit is earned, the faculty must be assured about the standards of quality of the off-campus endeavors—a frequent point of reservation and resistance. In-the-field supervisors have a somewhat different set of priorities and pressures than do academicians, and some sort of discussion between the groups is an important adjunct for underscoring the academic relevance of the experience gained away from the formal campus.

Universities got started, literally, as training programs for the priesthood. Over the years, the objectives shifted toward the educational benefits of "improving the mind and shaping character." Today, the pendulum is swinging back as many students, and their parents, give educational priority to preparation for a career. This conflict between vocational-professional training and liberal education is an old one. The Sophists started as true philosophers but later became teachers who made their living by traveling from town to town instructing students to be successful talkers, to be skilled performers of rhetoric to forward their careers in the Greek courts and assemblies. Truth and virtue got lost in the shuffle. Plato rescued education from this emphasis on technical (career) skills by awakening each student to his own powers, making students aware of the knowledge within themselves. This basic curricular issue of how best to balance education and training remains.

Teaching for career preparation makes some difference in what students learn and what they think about, but little difference in how they learn and think. The mental processes involved in acquiring knowledge are more general than the specific features making up the goals of instruction. Thus career orientation is more a curricular than an instructional issue. Courses in chemistry for nurses, statistics for business majors, psychology for lawyers, physics for physicians, and so forth cannot compromise what is good chemistry, statistics, psychology, or physics. The main emphasis is on the nature of the examples and applications rather than on the basic substance.

Students can compensate for weak classroom performance by the teacher, but have a dependent trust on what the teacher expects them to learn. Decisions about course content and its organization are made prior to the first day of class and reflect the depth and breadth of a teacher's understanding of the long-lasting relevance of selected information. The quality of these decisions is the first major component of good teaching. The content of most courses can be grouped into certain commonsense categories: facts, performance skills, concepts, methods, and values. Intermingled with all these recognized goals is the inevitable personal development of the individual student.

Information can be presented to students in many different ways. Lecturing is the most common and has certain advantages, but technological developments are further resources engaging students. These options will now be analyzed.

CHAPTER THREE

Options for Presenting Information

> Let him everyday say something, and even much,
> which, when the pupils hear, they may carry away
> with them, for though he may point out to them,
> in their course of reading, plenty of examples for
> their imitation, yet *the living voice,* as it is called,
> feeds the mind more nutritiously, and especially
> the voice of the teacher, whom his pupils, if they
> are but rightly instructed, both love and reverence.
> —Quintilian, *Institutes of Oratory*

The early teachers set a good example, but their task was uncomplicated by books, films, slides, tapes, and computers. They
told things to students, questions were asked back and forth,
and evaluative judgments were made. Walking through the
groves of Academe (the name of a Greek farmer), Plato quizzed
his students to expand their understanding of ideas already in
their minds. As a scientist, Galileo may have been out of line
with his observations about heavenly matters, but he was on tar-

get as a teacher when he said, "You cannot teach a man any-thing; you can only help him find it within himself." Today, we speak less of the "dialogue" than of "information processing," but the basics of instruction remain. This chapter will examine two options for presenting information—the lecture and tech-nological aids. The analysis is guided by how these presentations facilitate understanding on the part of the students, how they enhance motivation, learning, and the retention of knowledge.

The Teacher as a Lecturer

Most of us lecture most of the time, and we tend to get set in our ways; we develop habits of talking and patterns of movement, and we watch for cues about how we are doing. Lec-turing has become a security blanket without which we would neither feel like teachers nor be perceived by our students as such. The lecture—which took its name from a teacher of reli-gion and theology in the Middle Ages, the *lector,* a reader of lessons—became the chief form of instruction when teachers were, in fact, the main formal source of new information for students. The invention of the printing press in the fifteenth century and, more recently, the development of other media and computers have reduced dependence on the lecture as a source of information. The resiliency and the popularity of the lecture are justified. The teacher can be an inspirational force for students, an examiner of value judgments, and a source of the latest knowledge and a perspective of a topic. Sometimes the lecture is the single most effective method for arousing interest, initiating action, and challenging the attitudes and beliefs held by students.

The Manner of the Talking Teacher. Boredom is the ene-my of the lecture method. Other methods can also be boring—but with a less visible teacher to blame. To try to entertain is not, however, the appropriate alternative. Artificiality, role playing, and contrived efforts to arouse students cannot be sus-tained three hours a week throughout the term. The patronizing quality of such exhibitions counters credibility, and when credi-bility is lost, usefulness as a teacher is largely destroyed.

First, of course, the lecturer must be able to articulate a

point. Research analysis of students' ratings shows that students give central weight to how well the teacher talks (Kulik and McKeachie, 1975). Techniques of gesturing, eye contact, and use of the chalkboard help to direct and hold attention. Speaking with pear-shaped vowels and projecting one's voice to the back of the room are better than mumbling but will not, in themselves, promote learning. A polished performance may or may not be good teaching, as demonstrated by the "Dr. Fox" effect (Naftulin, Ware, and Connelly, 1973). Dr. Fox was an actor performing with style and flair as a guest lecturer, but he did not, in fact, have a message to give. Although he did not really make sense, the students probably assumed that he did and gave him good ratings as a teacher. In this contrived demonstration, advantage was being taken of the confidence held by students in a guest lecturer on "mathematical models of memory." He appeared to know what he was talking about, and his enthusiasm, though not his meaning, was contagious. Dr. Fox could not get away with this seductive trick day after day in the same class.

A good lecture requires considerable preparation, not so much in practicing and rehearsing one's style of presentation as in marking out the substance of the talk, its pacing, the sequence of points, and their integration with the lectures that preceded and those that will follow. Even so, it is not likely that a lecturer can control the direction of intellectual fixation for each student throughout a fifty-minute presentation. Students move in and out of rapt attention to the talker. Pacing is important because students are unlikely to understand topic B if they are still trying to grasp the meaning of topic A. They need an opportunity to catch up with the speaker; repetition, redundancy, and even silence may serve this purpose. A pause in the presentation is often refreshing since students cannot process information they hear with the same efficiency as when reading. The tightly packed lecture does not allow, as reading does, the dance of the eyes across the page to recover, examine, or confirm a questionable assertion or an uncertain point. Fast talking prohibits the scrutinizing and mulling over that make reading more active and analytical than listening.

Students appreciate knowing what their teachers believe

and how they arrive at these value judgments. Expressing the values embraced within a discipline not only enhances a teacher's credibility, it makes lectures more compelling. Students are responsive to the spontaneity and the serendipity that occur when a teacher is concentrating on the intellectual organization of a complex body of knowledge and its value implications.

In essence, therefore, the overriding consideration in lecturing is to have a point to make and to speak with credibility and enthusiasm. One's reputation among peers as a teacher reflects the public dimensions of classroom style—usually as a lecturer. Thus, to gain institutional recognition and reward, the teacher would do well to enhance competence in this mode of presenting information. Students are also sensitive to how lecturing helps them learn.

The View from the Other Side of the Lectern. Successful lecturing promotes the two basic conditions for learning and retention: motivation and meaning.

Techniques for motivating students differ, but one rule persists: Motivation is prerequisite for efficient learning, and good teaching transforms resistance to interest and sustains the curiosity that brought students into the course. The management of motivation requires adjustments to the differences in student interests, aims, and ambitions, just as good teaching responds to differences in the academic background, habits of study, and intellectual abilities of students.

Studies on college learning indicate that when lectures are arranged around questions that pique students' interest, learning is improved. Lectures that pose problems and actively involve students in their solutions are more likely to maintain and enhance motivation than are lectures that present neatly encapsulated principles and facts. Conceptual ordering can be exciting and is intrinsically more satisfying to students than overcoming the threat of a low grade or avoiding caustic comments from the teacher. A teacher's crutchlike dependency on extrinsic lures and threats for motivating learning ignores the intellectual curiosity of students and their desire to comprehend. This intrinsic satisfaction of understanding worthwhile material is the ideal motivating principle for guiding the organization of a lecture and its presentation. (See Chapter Four.)

Having announced the topic of the day, the main job is to present the arguments, the evidence to illustrate the points being made. The frequent use of examples, anecdotes, and personal speculations may stimulate students to construct their own bridges to test their ability to apply a principle to a specific event. Illustrative material not only gives pause but also provides instances that confirm (or deny) the extended meaning of the concept or theme under consideration. When substantive information is presented too fast, students have difficulty organizing a meaningful schema, but cognitive participation by students is important. When the lecturer overly controls the integrating process, students become passive listeners. Research has clearly shown that students learn better when they actively participate in the analysis of what is being said rather than passively accepting the conclusions (the meaning) of a distant speaker.

Long-term retention depends on how well students understand what is being lectured about. Understanding, in turn, depends on organizing this material into a personally meaningful form (see Chapters Five and Six). This integrating process is the means by which knowledge is stored in memory to become accessible later. A good lecture will stimulate students to be intellectually active, to filter and classify information, to integrate and elaborate ideas, to test themselves, and to speculate. This is the kind of cognitive processing going on inside the heads of students as they listen to their teacher covering the field.

Technological Aids

On occasion, media may serve as substitutes for the professor, but this is a left-handed way of teaching because it is important to integrate instructional technology with the live presentation and the other resources for teaching. Experienced teachers have learned how to make good use of the book—our most familiar and well-used technological aid. It serves as a useful model for examining the advantages and problems associated with machine-based means for teaching.

The Book. The spoken word floats and flees, but the

written word endures as the foundation technology for college instruction. It holds this position because *the reader is in control*—moving along, or back and forth, as fast or as slowly as needed to understand the message and to expand the reader's own ideas and images. Printed material is the primary resource to supplement the teacher or to be supplemented by the teacher. Earlier teachers had to defend access by students to the "limited editions" carefully guarded by the powers that be— mainly the church. It will be interesting to see how "safeguards" are placed for controlling access to computer-stored information (Nelkin, 1982).

Plato anticipated the instructional balance between the teacher and the book. In his discourse about the written word (between Socrates and Phaedrus), Plato drew the important distinction between the presentation of information and the analysis of its worth. We must remember that Socrates was a talker (teacher), not a writer (researcher), and there may be a touch of self-interest in this passage (*Phaedrus,* pp. 68-69):

> The fact is that this invention [the written word] will produce forgetfulness in the souls of those who have learned it. They will not need to exercise their memories, being able to rely on what is written, calling things to mind no longer from within themselves . . . . And as for wisdom, you're equipping your pupils with only a semblance of it, not with truth. Thanks to you and your invention, your pupils will be widely read without benefit of a teacher's instruction; in consequence, they'll entertain the delusion that they have wide knowledge, while they are, in fact, for the most part incapable of real judgment. They will also be difficult to get on with since they will have become wise merely in their own conceit, not genuinely so.

The message is clear: The educational potential of the printed word, other media, and the computer is best realized when the distinction is made between the presentation of information and how it is received and managed in a particular setting by the learner (Reiser and Gagné, 1983). Most technological devices were developed off campus and are promoted by people trying to sell something rather than to teach something. As an aid for instruction, the book, visual image, or computer program is important insofar as it elicits active responses from students, to help them find meaning within themselves.

The Visual Image. Mark Hopkins (president of Williams College, 1836-1872) made his local reputation as a teacher not by sitting at one end of a log, but by using the blackboard and other devices to stimulate "recitation" in his courses in physiology and philosophy (Jenness, 1964). The inventory of technological aids for instruction has expanded since Hopkins's day, but his purpose cannot be bettered if by "recitation" we mean active cognitive responding by students. A visual aid—film, slide, videotape, or overhead transparency—is not simply an "enriching learning experience" but specifically selected to promote understanding of particular points. Two instructional guides are in order:

1. Put the camera on the concept. In the earlier days of educational television, the camera was usually on the face of the talking teacher and less frequently was used to link the visual image with an idea. A film or set of slides may be an excellent means to magnify an object or event or to allow students visual access to places where the presence of an observer might be distracting or hazardous, but mainly the image should contribute to making a point, to enhancing the understanding of concepts, principles, procedures, and themes significant to a particular course (Gagné, 1980). The camera is on the concept while the talking teacher—before, during, or after the showing—points out how the visual representation supports and confirms the meaning of something larger than what is specifically seen on the screen. A technological aid is just that—a resource used by the teacher to add clarity and meaning to a conceptual objective planned in advance by the teacher.

2. View and review. The replay of the visual image, like turning back a page, allows the student to control the presentation and to review, literally, visual material not yet understood.

With the repeat-viewing capability, tapes can carry information of high density because students are able to peel off layers of meaning in successive viewings. Closed-circuit television never amounted to much as a condition for learning because a student's only option was to struggle along with the class or to mentally turn it off. Both teacher and student gain from decentralized control; students need the flexibility to adapt to the stimulus material within their own pace of learning, and teachers need the flexibility to select media-based material in support of a particular goal or subgoal of the course. A teacher's hand-drawn chalkboard sketch or self-produced videotape is more likely to clarify or elaborate a lecture topic than is a commercially produced item. Today's students have been viewing commercial television for most of their lives and may squirm when shown a homemade videotape, but they will appreciate, just the same, their teacher's effort in preparing a relevant message for viewing by a given class.

A vital part of learning is sometimes carried by audio cues. A medical student cannot learn to discriminate heart sounds by reading or watching oscilloscope tracings alone. Poetry listening adds something to poetry reading. Drama heard is usually better than drama read. The audio room in the library is designed as a place where students can listen to material made available by the teacher to serve particular instructional purposes. In general, however, adults can process information faster and better via the eye than the ear, and the attention span for listening is reduced without visual support.

The Teacher and Computers

This section stems from an area of great activity but makes only one basic point: The mature development of computing technology as an educational resource rests on contributions from teachers of particular subjects. Computing is well established in research, in administrative data processing, and in our libraries. Potentially, it is a comparable resource for college-level instruction, and isolated examples, here and there, confirm this promise. How fast it becomes such a resource depends in large measure on direct involvement by teachers in helping to transform a discipline's language into the language of the machine and then into a language appropriate for students.

In the beginning—about twenty years ago—computer-assisted instruction was a rigidly programmed question-and-answer arrangement. Since that time, hardware and software developments have extended this technology toward the instructional diversity required for the education of college students. Computer literacy is growing as students in many high schools and college departments are learning about the principles, procedures, and uses of computing. A number of factors, however, hold back the more rapid advance of instructional computing as a means of learning substantive material. High cost is one, and while the purchase price of the machines themselves is going down, simply staying up to date is expensive. Successive generations of equipment move by quickly. Research and development costs in the software domain must also be included—constant changes in terminal capabilities, programming languages, expanded memories, revised course materials, and integration with other instructional resources, for example, videodiscs.

It sounds defeating, but progress is being made. When our grandchildren go to college, they will feel as comfortable with this technology as we do with a book—including studying via a computer in the shade of a tree. But between now and then much needs to be done by computing engineers, by educational research and development specialists, and especially by those teachers who take a positive and constructive view of instructional computing rather than putting it down as another threat to their own security and status. The advent of a new instructional technology is usually met with resistance. Raben (1983, p. 27), a professor of English, encourages us to take a positive view toward computers. He concluded a delightful statement about the "advent of the post-Gutenberg university": "For centuries, we have extolled the responsiveness of the human teacher. We then added the extensive information available in the printed book. Lately we have been impressed with the ability of the phonograph record, tape, and film to repeat endlessly the same oral/visual material without fatigue, or to replay selected sections on command. In the microcomputer and its peripheral equipment, we finally have come a long step closer to combining these qualities in a single entity that may begin to approximate the perfect teacher."

Teachers must prepare themselves to enter the system, to program the computer in anticipation of the kinds of responses that might be expected from students studying a subject that teachers know best (Gagné, 1982). I stress teacher because such a "programmer" is aware of the kinds of problems typically encountered with certain topics or units of study and the kind of "feedback" that will establish understanding. The programming contribution of the teacher is necessary because, in contrast to books and other media, the computer is reactive; it responds to answers and decisions made by the student working at the terminal. This reactive capability tests a student's response against a preformed (programmed) criterion or standard of what is "right" or "wrong."

In the simplest case, the computer presents a question, the student responds, and the computer immediately reacts with confirming information or indicates what corrections or further inquiries might be in order—including the ever-present bailout, "The computer is not programmed for your response; try something different." This interactive mode can be exceedingly complex as students working with a simulation program, for example, immediately come to grips with elements that are essential for solving a problem. Computer-based simulation programs are vital contributions from teachers, who can, for example, create plans for new highways, produce environmental impact analyses, map production lines, detail robot functions, make economic projections, search for a medical diagnosis, and design a research project.

Publication of research and scholarship earns stronger recognition than does preparation of audiovisual media or computer materials for purposes of instruction. Teachers have the talent, but the will is weak when they see the grass is greener in pastures other than "authoring" a teaching machine. This constraint will remain until the rewards for writing a program approach the recognition given to writing a textbook or syllabus.

In any event, the exciting potential of instructional computing will not be realized until teachers write programs appropriate to what they teach.

Looking Back and Looking Ahead

It is sometimes hard to see the classroom for the devices; they come and go, making it difficult to keep instructional technology in perspective.

Lessons Learned. All kinds of instructional fads and fancies move in and out of the campus, but technological aids persist. We have learned certain lessons about the interchange between college teaching and the world of media and computers:

1. The most important single change in the progress in instructional technology is its decentralized capability, from massive classroom presentation to portable cassettes and personal (mini-, micro-, home) computers. Wherever an electrical outlet (and, perhaps, a telephone jack) is found, a study site can be set up with the learner in control.
2. Teachers will default the educational uses of technology if they leave this resource to those less able to provide forceful units of instruction. Teachers of specific fields must generate more of the materials presented by automated devices—and keep these programs up to date.
3. A particular technological arrangement can nearly always be found to provide worthwhile supplements to a conventional classroom presentation. Local programs of training for the faculty will facilitate the effective use of technological aids that, in turn, must be readily available at no cost to the teacher.

Looking Ahead. Here is an interesting question: What will be the role of the professor when the world of organized knowledge is, literally, at the fingertips of students? Certain basic functions of teaching will surely persist:

1. Selective retrieval—teachers must guide students to select and scan material from multiple sources of information—

think of the Yellow Pages times N-degrees of complexity (Stoan, 1982). Complex files of information can be presented from computer memories and interlocking retrieval systems, and students need help in knowing which buttons to push when entering this electronic world of stored information.

2. Value judgments—knowledge in the absence of values is only a status symbol. Information is neutral and technology is amoral, but how they are used is not. The whole educational enterprise is interlaced with value judgments as a system of checks and balances in the social uses of available knowledge (Rosenbaum and others, 1983).

3. Problem solving—the methods and techniques of solving problems will continue to be a difficult topic of instruction. The demonstration by the faculty of originality; insight; creative expressions in teaching, research, and scholarship; and problem solving will remain the marks of academic leadership and, at the same time, serve as models for students seeking to do likewise.

4. Evaluation—the evaluating function of the teacher will be more complex in the years ahead. The scoring key for testing will go beyond assessing informational accuracy by including criteria relating to how accumulated knowledge might be used. Assuming that our anchoring principle—academic freedom—stands firm, value judgments will be placed squarely on the table for analysis and evaluation.

The lecturing teacher has adapted to the book as a technological resource for education, and now audiovisual media and computers are becoming more accessible as supplements for the classroom analysis of knowledge. Technology may have the effect of decentralizing the campus to home, work place, and study centers, but at any site, instruction cannot get too far away from the essential conditions for motivation, learning, and memory. What students learn and what they think about have changed during the time of recorded history, but evolution has not had time to change how the mind works, how it comprehends the meaning of signs, symbols, signals, and cues given by the saber-toothed tiger, the medicine man, the printed page, or the computer display.

The stimulus source of information is not a critical element in comparison to the meaning students give to a presentation, the feelings aroused, and how knowledge is used to satisfy curiosity and to solve problems. The effective use of the various options for presenting information puts pressure on the teacher to probe the meaning and implications of a unit of knowledge, to be a mentor in learning and in the forming of value judgments. In whatever instructional setting, the first charge to the teacher is to get and to hold the attention of students because interest (motivation) is a prerequisite condition for effective learning.

CHAPTER FOUR

Generating Enthusiasm to Learn

For as long as the responses of men and women are complicated and personal, the successful teacher, the teacher who is influential, who is remembered, will succeed by the power of contagion, by transmitting to his pupils directly, in a thousand subtle ways, his seriousness about his subject, his enthusiasm for it. His secret will not be chiefly inventiveness and originality in the presentation of material (though these are virtues), nor in his histrionic power (though this may serve him well), but in the daily demonstration that nothing on earth means more to him than living the life of the mind, in learning, searching, testing, proving, in developing delicacy of perception and the habit of disciplined thought.   —Professor emeritus of English language and literature

The literature about motivation meanders, but certain checkpoints are relevant to how teachers and students do their work in the classroom and at the study desk. The direction and the strength of effort are influenced by many affective states—feelings, interests, curiosities, anxieties, values, and aspirations—and the motivational profile differs for each person. Speculations range far about why people do this and that, and sometimes we pause to examine our own motives. In any event, motivational matters are always present and cannot be set aside if we want to understand what is going on in the classroom.

Instruction and Motivation

Going to college is the realization of a plan that, for most students, started many grades ago; they were motivated to do well when they first walked onto the campus. A closer look, however, is needed regarding the motivation to achieve the aims of a given course of study. Motivation is prerequisite to learning, and a teacher can flounder by ignoring or misreading cues about the task-related motivation of students. Nevertheless, the factor of motivation is often downplayed as being a lower-order form of pedagogy—"My job is to teach my subject and if students don't want to learn, that's their problem." This defensive stance about motivation is countered by teachers' own enthusiasm for their subjects.

College teachers have close identity with their field and hold their subjects near and dear. These positive attitudes show through and have a powerful influence on the motivation of their students. Enthusiasm is contagious and, as the course proceeds, students will begin to understand and appreciate the love affair their teacher is having with statistics, microbiology, Middle English prose, or calculus. This genuine conviction about the worth of a given unit of knowledge and the curiosity to know more are prime instructional resources; imitations emerge —what the teacher values, students begin to value—and motivation has taken root.

It is unfortunate when teachers are assigned to teach a subject for which they feel little enthusiasm or interest; their negative attitudes show through. The teachers receive their pay, but such extrinsic rewards do not bring out the best in teachers, just as grades do not bring out the best in students. A better motivational climate prevails when teaching reflects a genuine excitement about the subject matter. Students respond to the spontaneous indicators of value and are, indeed, "observing the scholarly mind at work"—not only what the teacher knows but also why she has such excitement about a particular topic. The ability to start this motivational chain reaction is characteristic of good teaching. In fact, McKeachie (1974, p. 10) holds that, "probably no one thing is more important in education than the teacher's enthusiasm and energy."

The hierarchy of motivational problems ranges from discipline to inspiration, from encouraging slow learners to setting a challenge for fast learners. The heart of the matter, from day to day, is to guide students toward understanding the meaning of a particular array of facts, procedures, and ideas. You want this information to stick to the ribs of students as being something they should learn and learn well. Telling them this will not make it so, but students are interested to know why—the perennial motivation question—it is judged to be so important. Knowing what the teacher cares about helps to direct and sustain the motivation of students. When the dynamics of the student are in tune with the teacher, intellectual correspondence soon follows.

The false connection between entertainment and motivation is one reason for faculty resistance to issues of motivation. Experienced teachers know that there are far better ways to motivate students than to make them chuckle—that a student-based popularity poll might be a superficial measure of good teaching. Demonstrating Plato's love of good ideas will have a lasting effect and is in line with the serious motivational purpose of enhancing students' efforts to learn and remember.

Motivation and Learning

Investigators have developed productive means for examining the invisible relations between motivation and learning. Two research-based concepts are especially useful for understanding and managing the dynamics of the learning process: reinforcement and curiosity.

Reinforcement. Under a variety of labels—from hedonism

to feedback to love—the principle of reinforcement has been used the world over to account for how behavior changes as a function of experience (learning). Psychologists certainly did not discover this phenomenon but recognized its potential for understanding the nature of how learning proceeds. Their analyses in the research laboratory specify the particular conditions that influence reinforcing effects and identify subprinciples that might be applicable to practical problems of teaching and learning.

Pavlov started things off with his formulation of the conditioned response—a tightly controlled pattern of stimulus-response learning. For him, reinforcement had little to do with motivation but was defined by the association of events along the time line—the principle of *contiguity* earlier set forth by Aristotle, John Locke, and others. A major conceptual change was made in the 1930s by Clark Hull at Yale; his research and theory made motivation ("drive reduction") the critical factor in reinforcement. In this sense, Hull's view was in parallel with the earlier position of Edward L. Thorndike's Law of Effect, which held that learning is a function of the pleasant, satisfying consequences of a response. B. F. Skinner was the next landmark theorist, as he extended the views of Hull and Thorndike by developing the concept of reinforcement as the dominant factor in the analysis of behavior.

Basic and applied research on reinforcement confirms the dominance of reward over punishment. This reminder is relevant to instruction because it is so easy to make comments that are critical, negative, caustic, and threatening about what a student believes, says, and does. A direct or implied putdown to a student can quickly undo the tenuous allegiance and feelings of identification toward the teacher and the area of knowledge he or she represents. The main effect of punishment is to curtail, constrain, or simply block a particular response. The consequences are likely to be frustration, anxiety, and negative attitudes. When a student is learning simple perceptual-motor skills, punishment—to be effective—should immediately follow the execution of the wrong response. Students at the college level can, of course, bridge time with their own thinking; they can conceptually recreate the original setting to which the punishment (or reward) now accrues. Punishment, however, does not give explicit and constructive information to the learner about what redirections should be taken—the essential purpose of teaching.

The teacher's practical problem is one of finding suitable techniques for meting out rewards and punishment. The principle of reinforcement is exercised in many different ways. Carl Rogers, a humanist psychologist, and Skinner, a behaviorist, were frequent adversaries. Rogers' basic dictum, "unconditional positive regard" between therapist and client (patient), can be interpreted as confirming the "molding and shaping" effects of reinforcement. Silence can be quite punishing, and a patronizing "stroke" (praise) may backfire as being equally aversive. Nonverbal cues are reacted to by students in terms of their positive and negative implications. Thinking back about influential teachers we have known usually brings to mind persons who gave accent to the positive—not necessarily providing a steady diet of honey but, on balance, more reward than punishment.

Reinforcement is a pervasive component of instruction. Insofar as students derive primary satisfaction from a course of study, secondary reinforcing effects occur. Heretofore neutral signs, signals, and labels become associated with and sustain this positive affective state, which extends to a student's identification with a discipline field. The voice quality and other manners of the teacher are associated with these positive feelings about a teacher and a course. Secondary reinforcement is a good account of the modeling influence of the teacher.

Schedules of reinforcement have long been studied in the laboratory. So far as teaching is concerned, a significant finding is the holding power of being reinforced only once in a while—the slot-machine or patient fisherman phenomenon. For reasons that are still a matter of theoretical debate, material learned under conditions of aperiodic reinforcement remains in memory better than if it were learned under constant or regular reinforcement. Information from the teacher that the student is correct need not be given after every response. The information students learn should be organized in such a way that, on occasion, they will have an experience that reconfirms the meaning of this information. One explanation for the high rate of forgetting what was once read or heard is that this information is never, or rarely, reinforced by subsequent events in the student's life; the probabilities for aperiodic reinforcement are low.

The early development of reinforcement technology relied heavily on extrinsic contingencies between a response and its consequences. With the teaching machine, for example, students pressed buttons, turned knobs, checked boxes, or underlined specific words and did, in fact, learn what this machine was programmed to teach. It was soon discovered, however, that the feedback given by the device came too late to make much of a difference. Having read a carefully worded and sequenced statement, the college student immediately sensed that the material was understood and thus was already reinforced by the time the machine gave its signal.

To think of reinforcement as the management of extrinsic rewards and punishment—carrots and sticks—is to ignore the power of intrinsic reinforcement. This principle has high relevance to understanding the effects of instruction and the private process of learning. As students read books, they have a reassuring feeling of understanding and go forward, or they sense confusion and go back to reread parts that they select in order to straighten things out. A well-organized course increases the probability that the individual student will experience the intrinsic satisfaction of knowing that he or she is moving along the right track. Managing information and gaining understanding are, in the long run, their own best reward.

Our crutchlike dependency on grading as the dominant means of motivational control leads us to overlook the ubiquitous nature of intrinsic reinforcement. We underestimate its pervasive nature if we think of reinforcement as being dependent on what the teacher gives the student in the form of extrinsic rewards. For example, when a student puts a term paper on the teacher's desk, most of the educational value of that exercise in reading, writing, and thinking has already been accomplished. The teacher's marginal comments and the grade marked on the cover page are relatively minor reinforcing events compared to the student's own positive feelings at having put together a well-ordered flow of ideas.

The campus is loaded with reinforcing states of affairs, and teachers and students have a language for reporting these effects: challenged by, excited by, turned on or turned off, pleased with, satisfied about, and comfortable with. Little is added by actually using the term "reinforcement," but it is a good concept here for analyzing the basics of instruction; it helps us to understand an otherwise seemingly random sequence of motivating conditions and events.

Curiosity to Know. Intellectual curiosity is the ideal motive for instruction. When curiosity is nourished, reinforcement is in good hands—the satisfaction students gain from learning about what they want to know. Students come to the first day of class wondering what lies ahead. They have interests to nourish, values to examine, informational gaps to fill, and beliefs to strengthen. Each is a bundle of propelling expectations and curiosities. These interests are not worn on the sleeve but in a quiet way selectively set the stage for what they hear and see and how they think. In 1693, John Locke admonished teachers to take curiosity into account. It could hardly be better stated by a cognitive theorist, a behaviorist, or a humanist today:

> Not to check or discountenance any Enquiries he shall make, nor suffer them to be laugh'd at; but to answer all his Questions, and explain the Matters, he desires to know, so as to make them as much intelligible to him as suits the capacity of his Age and Knowledge. Mark what 'tis his Mind aims at in the Question, and not what Words he expresses it in: And when you have informed and satisfied him in that, you shall see how his Thoughts will enlarge themselves, and how by fit Answers he may be led on farther than perhaps you could imagine. For Knowledge is grateful to the Understanding, as Light to the Eyes. . . . But had they been treated with more kindness and Respect, and their Questions answered, as they should, to their

satisfaction; I doubt not but they would have taken more pleasure, in learning and improving their knowledge [(1693) 1964, p. 89].

Poorly motivated students—at least those uninterested in learning what we have to teach—sit before us all the time. Whatever the causes of the indifference might be, the teacher is the person to initiate corrective action by arousing and sustaining some degree of curiosity. Given the constraining realities of mass instruction, it is difficult to build on what each student might want to know. The straightforward announcement, "This material will be covered on the next examination," is a much easier way to stimulate and sustain the interests of a classroom full of students. They do work hard for grades, to win special honors, and to meet the requirements for graduation, but the lasting educational effect of these extrinsic motives is trivial compared to what students learn in response to their own curiosities and aspirations.

Self-esteem stands high on the hierarchy of student motives, and self-regulating drives, such as the need to achieve success, to avoid failure, and to gain the feeling of competence and mastery, are usually available as resources to be tapped by the teacher. On occasion, direct forms of ego-massage may be appropriate, but to make self-fulfillment itself an explicit aim is something other than teaching. The better instructional route is to focus on the subject matter and to depend on the satisfaction of competence and mastery to serve the self-enhancing purposes of students.

The Motivation to Remember

Students complain that teachers stress memorizing over understanding, but the store of knowledge in memory that is tapped in trivial recollections is also used for making wise decisions. In a technical sense, learning and memory are intertwined since the initial process of learning involves the carryover of one experience to the next; the learner does better on Trial 2 for having remembered what happened on Trial 1. Weak original learning is not compensated by strong remembering.

Selective perception—we see what we are looking for—is an ever-present dynamic when the student starts to study, to listen to a lecture, to initiate a laboratory exercise, or to make observations on a field trip. Whether a student is learning something new or retrieving something old, a screening and filtering process reflects the intentions and interests (motives) of the individual student. Further, these affective factors influence how the store of information in memory is recombined for making a final judgment. This motivation-cognition interaction is the means by which each student sustains meaning and continuity from one minute of study to the next, from one class period to the next, and from one year to the next.

In the absence of getting and holding attention, instruction is futile. In one way or another—for example, "now hear this"—the teacher initiates a selective set toward the topic at hand, to direct attention to the information that, by precept, is about to be laid before the class. Note, however, that the quality of the initial set taken by students is also influenced by the enthusiasm evidenced in the teacher's opening remarks about the topic of the day. This initial motivational climate is, of course, inevitably screened and modified by the selective factors within each student. Only certain words are registered in short-term memory, and from there they are reorganized in long-term memory. Again, meaning derives from what the student already knows and cares about. Comprehension does not emerge full blown but accumulates in fits and starts as the student intermingles the information coming in with the dual factors of interest and ideas already in mind. These personal revisions continue as experience continues.

The *qualitative* changes in the retention of earlier events have been the subject of considerable research. The classic book *Remembering,* by the English psychologist F. C. Bartlett (1932), examined the retention of visual images as well as prose. He found, for example, that features which seem incongruent or inconsistent are leveled out by the recaller, key items are sharpened in one way or another, and the whole episode is assimilated into the teller's repertoire of knowledge, beliefs, and values.

This reshuffling of the materials in memory is automatic and is intrinsic to almost every complex cognitive event. A student's current inventory of values, interests, motives, and aspirations controls the integration between what is being studied here and now and what went on before. Memory is malleable and easily altered by the selective and filtering interplay of motives and the information in memory store; this is why "a twice-told tale never loses." Only on occasion do recollections knowingly take these changes into account. We feel uncomfortable with informational gaps or with loose ends dangling, and so it is normal and inevitable that qualitative changes in memory will occur as a function, in part, of motivating factors.

Robert Zajonc (1980, p. 154) marshaled an impressive array of data to underscore the intimacy between affective states and intellectual decision making: "In fact, it is entirely possible that the very first stage of the organism's reaction to stimuli and the very first elements in retrieval are affective. It is further possible that we can like something or be afraid of it before we know precisely what it is . . . and when we try to recall, recognize, or retrieve an episode, a person, a piece of music, a story, a name, in fact, anything at all, the affective quality of the original input is the first element to emerge." Lazarus (1982) differs in emphasis but confirms the view that thinking and feeling are never far apart.

Instruction for purposes of remembering is a two-part process: the intellectual treatment of information while indicating its worth. The attachment of an idea to the feeling that it is worthwhile condenses the meaning of the material and sets it up in long-term memory. The teacher moves back and forth between the cognitive and the affective domains, and the motivational side of teaching is every bit as complicated and diverse as the intellectual aspects of the task.

Entering students start with a loose array of interests and ambitions, but things tighten up in the classroom where motivation is geared to learning particular topics placed before them. The enthusiasm of the teacher toward the subject at hand helps to set the motivational climate; this unforced display of interests, positive attitudes, and enduring values are signs to students about what is worth knowing and retaining in their own store of knowledge. Motivation is an integral factor in learning, memory, thinking, and kindred cognitive events and is, therefore, an indispensable resource to be influenced by the teacher. Two major motivation-linked concepts pervade the instructional scene: reinforcement and intellectual curiosity. The intrinsic reinforcing effects of satisfying curiosity are educationally more powerful than extrinsic rewards of, for example, grades and honors. The dynamics of memory produce a constant reshuffling of what is in memory store, and selective recall is just as real as is selective perception. Being involved with motivational matters is an inevitable part of the teacher's job.

Students learn what they care about and remember what they understand. The first half of this proposition was the theme of the present chapter; the second half is underlined by the next chapter.

CHAPTER FIVE

Remembering Follows Understanding

The highest law and guiding light, the center and circumference, the foundation and summit of the art of teaching, is this alone: Teach everything through examples, precepts, and use or imitation. That is, always place the material of instruction before the student's eyes and explain what you have put before him; as for the student, when he has had the material explained and understands it, let him try to express it in a variety of forms until he can reproduce it perfectly.

—Comenius, *General Didactics*

Research findings are clear in showing that the conditions that promote sound original learning also enhance retention and recall. Motivation is one of these conditions, and a second is meaningfulness—what students understand. When people complain about having a "poor memory" for names, dates, and procedural sequences, they are indicating a weakness with respect to how they perceived the worth and the meaning of such items at the time they were first encountered; the *motivation* to establish significant *meaning* was weak.

Memory is a broad concept; scientists study memory from the molecule to society. The dramatic display of special feats of memory grabs our attention, but as Ericsson and Chase (1982, pp. 614-615) observe, "Exceptional memory is a skill based on learned cognitive processes, developed through extensive practice and experience. . . . In every recorded feat of exceptional memory we have identified the same components: the importance of prior experience and practice, the availability of meaningful associations, storage in LTM [long-term memory], and efficient retrieval of information from LTM. A single model is adequate to describe all adult memory." Contemporary research and theory about memory are part and parcel of cognitive theory—the role of memory in comprehending new information, its retention, and recall (diSibio, 1982). Thus, recalling past events is only one aspect of memory because in its more technical meaning, memory is involved in the perception of things and in sustaining the continuity from one experience to another. Memory is the mind at work. These pages will emphasize what teachers do toward helping students use their own resources for storing knowledge in long-term memory and being able to retrieve this information later in quite different settings.

The Interlock Between Rehearsal and Retention

Rehearsing is ubiquitous, pervasive, and key to gaining understanding and for retention. By various overt and covert processes—reviewing, practicing, organizing, and reorganizing information—the meaning of a unit of information is established in memory. Research on short-term memory, for example, finds that we rehearse the item during the first few seconds after receiving a bit of information. We have learned from experience, for example, that when introduced to a stranger, we should repeat the person's name to fix this identification in memory. A rehearsal may simply mimic the stimulus item or may group, classify, and pattern the information into a more meaningful unit. The last four digits in the telephone number 663-1776 are immediately "chunked" as a date already having meaning;

it needs less rehearsal than some numbers to become fixed (encoded) in memory.

Understanding sometimes comes quickly but not in the absence of prior effort to review background information relevant to the sudden solution of a problem. Insight, discovery, and "eureka" are end products of considerable mental activity.

The Active Search for Meaning. How does a word, phrase, sentence, paragraph, symbol, or pattern of symbols take on meaning? This epistemological question has a long history with many answers. From Aristotle to John Locke to twentieth-century psychology, the laws of association were usually given as the answers—acquiring new stimulus-response connections. This behavioral approach never did seem to account adequately for the complexity, the diversity, the mystery of human thinking. Contemporary research and theory on the "higher mental processes"—cognitive theory—address more forthrightly how the individual encodes, stores, and retrieves information. This chapter emphasizes the role of rehearsal as students search for and acquire meaning.

Early in the nineteenth century, Johann Herbart, a philosopher, coined "apperceptive mass" in reference to the sum of one's background of knowledge and capabilities. Each student comes to class with a repertoire of information, ideas, facts, beliefs, and skills (manipulative and conceptual) that serve as the frame of reference, the context, within which new information and events are perceived. The general skill of reading, for example, transcends the specifics of a particular sequence of words; the accomplished chess player responds to perceptual patterns that are not yet there; the doctor perceives a new patient against sets of diagnostic and therapeutic concepts. A good reader abstracts, elaborates, and paraphrases the gist of a metaphor's meaning. Each of these activities illustrates the figure-ground relationship; that is, the meaning of a perceived particular is influenced by the background of experiences accumulated by each learner.

Perceived meaning is personal and subjective as each student combines new events with the long-term store of information in memory. This integration is distinctive for each student and carries an idiosyncratic quality. Meaning is never exactly the same from one person to the next, and the individual student, therefore, is the de facto unit of instruction.

Memory and Meaning. College credit is being earned these days in some weird and wondrous ways: snorkeling in a tropical reef, mountain climbing, winter camping, backpacking through the desert, and kayaking down a white-water river. Apart from questions of academic relevance, it is a good bet that these experiences will be remembered a long time. These students walked, swam, and paddled one day after the next and verbally recounted their experiences in the evening. The study of academic subjects may not be quite so exhilarating, but the effects of rehearsing are the same: to establish meaning and continuity to a successive chain of words, symbols, and observations. Assigning a sequence of homework problems is an assignment to rehearse.

Researchers differentiate short-term from long-term memory. The former refers to only the first few seconds as incoming information is being encoded as, for example, when we carry a telephone number from the directory to the dial—while rehearsing along the way. Long-term memory is the store of knowledge, the frame of reference, the context, the integrating base for making new information meaningful. (Over the years, research on human learning has established certain words as having an absolutely fundamental reference—such as *meaningful, reinforcement, self-esteem,* and *motivation.* Despite its overuse and distortion in media discourse—the "meaningful relationship" in a soap opera—the term remains in these pages. I can avoid *innovative, communicate, input,* and *growing concerns,* but not *meaningful.*)

The interlock among motivation, memory, and meaning derives from rehearsal on the part of the student. Some signs of this activity are external—that is, speaking, problem solving, writing, and other forms of overt action—but internal, covert effort is also necessary for meaning and is probably more extensive. Bransford (1979) demonstrated how comprehension of prose is influenced by linking specific items of information within an integrating theme already in memory store. Read the following passage with the expectation of recalling it later:

The procedure is actually quite simple. First you arrange items into different groups. Of course one pile may be sufficient depending on how much there is to do. . . . It is important not to overdo things. That is, it is better to do too few things at once than too many. In the short run this may not seem important, but complications can easily arise. A mistake can be expensive as well. . . . It is difficult to foresee any end to the necessity for this task in the immediate future, but then, one never can tell. After the procedure is completed, one arranges the materials into different groups again. Eventually they will be used once more and the whole cycle will then have to be repeated. However, that is part of life [Bransford, 1979, pp. 134–135].

The words and sentences make partial sense, but the whole passage would be easier to understand and remember if the reader first knew it was about washing clothes. Advance knowledge of the integrating theme provides continuity and meaning to the sequence of sentences and hence promotes better recall of the gist of the theme. This simple demonstration illustrates a fundamental principle: The initial meaning of information and its later recall are influenced by the prior knowledge (memory) students bring to bear to the material at hand. "Paying attention" means that students are actively combining what is coming in with what they already know; they are rehearsing for purposes of understanding and thus to remember the topic under review. It follows that a teacher should be explicit about the theme for integrating the specifics composing the day's lecture and make frequent references to this conceptual signpost.

Instructional Guides to Enhance Long-Term Memory

The instructional use of two principles will upgrade the quality and the amount of information retrieved from long-term memory: active participation and overlearning.

Active Participation When Learning. In one way or another, nearly every treatise about schoolroom learning refers to the importance of active participation by the student. This global prescription is well founded on research and confirmed by practical experience. The most common objection to the lecture method, for example, is the passive posture taken by students. When attending to a good lecture, students are actively integrating, organizing, and elaborating the information being talked about; they are rehearsing.

Rehearsing is essentially what students do at the study desk. They have the flexibility to select material needing analysis and review and to set the pace of rehearsal. Rehearsal often involves the use of mnemonic schemes to strengthen rote memory. These aids apply more to remembering a specific event, episodic memory, than to comprehending the internal structure of a unit of information (Bellezza, 1981). In Chapter Two, these aids were judged to be more relevant to factual learning than to the comprehension of concepts; certainly, students do not need mnemonic aids to help them remember what they really care about—their values. Some sort of cognitive cuing device may be helpful for remembering where you parked your car or how far along you are when running or swimming laps, but students must come directly to grips with the intrinsic meaning of the ideas handled in a college course. At this level of learning, leave the mnemonic crutches aside.

Noam Chomsky (1972) drew the important distinction between "surface structure"—the words themselves—and "deep structure"—their meaning to the individual. A student can rehearse at either level or meld the two. Imagery may also be part of the picture. If asked to recall one's first Christmas away from home, the details of persons, place, and feelings come roaring back into awareness. The material seems to have been resting in memory waiting for an excuse to come forward. However, most of what we perceive in the passing scene goes in one eye and out the other; the parade of events serves no personal interest and is not encoded into a meaningful unit of experience. Isolated perceptions simply do not last long in memory unless, of course, this isolation is itself a distinctive cue. In any case, the fact of recall is evidence that the learner has, someplace down the line, been busy rehearsing a particular item of experience into meaningful shape.

Overlearning. Overlearning means to continue studying (rehearsal) beyond the least demanding criterion of success. Having achieved one perfect repetition, for example, practice continues until no errors occur on ten successive trials. The research analysis of overlearning indicates why this extended rehearsal pays retention dividends.

Mechanical drilling and verbatim memorizing aim at the narrow encoding of surface material. A more efficient use of rehearsal effort is to extend the boundaries of what is being learned. That is, the breadth of meanings can be increased by placing a specific item of information within a sequence of several different contexts or frames of reference. All of this variable encoding increases the probability that the learner will recognize the relevance of a given fact, concept, or procedure when retrieval is called for in a different setting than when originally learned. Overlearning increases the variety and complexity of the figure-ground relationship; it establishes a broader base of meaning. A successful student in statistics will see the concept of correlation as applicable to a wide range of conditions in the sciences, society, and the life of an individual; the idea has breadth of meaning.

This degree of comprehension also requires that the student dig down into the deep structure to integrate the new stimulus material with already meaningful units of information. Students studying for an objective examination are more likely to stay near surface meanings, to recognize the words and symbols, rather than to derive the gist of the deeper meaning and to paraphrase this meaning in preparation for answering a penetrating question on an essay examination. Repeated rehearsal—overlearning—is the means whereby the learner contributes breadth (variability) and depth (level of analysis) in constructing an enduring understanding of what the topics, the ideas, and the procedures are all about. Overlearning establishes a diversity of cognitive cues for retrieving this vital information at some later time away from the classroom.

Cramming before a test is the usual practice by students, and while it may result in a satisfactory test performance, a rapid rate of forgetting thereafter is a likely result. If students would distribute their study (rehearsal) effort over a period of time, their retention would be much better. A four-hour study period will, for example, be more effective for retention if spaced into two or more periods of concentrated effort. I have been making this admonition to students for many years but few change their study habits. Since students do study for tests, frequent quizzes encourage the distribution of rehearsal effort. Another supporting approach is to make homework assignments in a pattern that leads to spaced study effort, that is, the recall and reanalysis of information learned earlier in the term. The spaced-effort phenomenon is real enough and, over the years, scholars have noted the constructive effects of an incubation period in seeking a solution to a problem. What happens by way of cognitive processing during the rest interval is a matter for speculation; the pragmatic effect will have to suffice.

Testing for What Is in Memory. Students test their own understanding of what they have learned as they complete assignments, write term papers, and participate in group discussions. Formal testing by teachers is a more complicated matter and is, at best, a sampling of what students know. The inability to recall is by no means proof that the material is not locked up someplace in memory waiting for the right cues to release it. "Recognition" memory is commonly observed as better than "recall" memory. Thus an objective examination emphasizing a student's ability to recognize material will show higher retention than a test of recall—filling in the blank spaces. The most sensitive measure of retention is the effort needed to relearn the original material. Usually, a significant savings occurs during relearning showing that the initial ordering (processing) of information leaves its trace. These conclusions are confounded by the fact that the testing process itself serves as a quick rehearsal opportunity. Chapter Nine returns to this problem of assessing how well certain topics have been learned.

The Mechanics of Forgetting

Sound original learning and good intentions to remember notwithstanding, forgetting does take place; at least, we and our students are unable to recall as needed. Over the past 100 years, a steady research effort has been directed at the nature of forgetting, and we now understand its complexities a little better than formerly.

The folk theory about forgetting is uncomplicated: Unused facts, ideas, and skills gradually fade away with the passage of time. This disuse theory fails, however, to explain too many commonplace observations. For example, why do some items fade more quickly than others, and why do we suddenly recall names and other "forgotten" events? Information does not just peter out through lack of use; the original learning was weak or something happened to block or interfere with the cues for the retrieval of material from the long-term store in memory. The psychoanalytical concept of repression likewise does not offer sufficient detail to account for the differential effects seen as students struggle to remember particular items at testing time. In contrast to the global and somewhat circular psychoanalytical reasoning based on clinical observations, the findings from experimental studies in the laboratory and in the classroom point to instructional steps the teacher can take to forestall (to some extent) the mental breakdown called forgetting.

Forgetting as an Effect of Interference. The well-established interference theory was a landmark development in understanding the intrinsic relations between learning and memory. Literally hundreds of experiments have explored variations of its primary thesis: Forgetting is a consequence of interfering effects, that is, the consequence of normal activities such as reading, listening, observing, and being intellectually awake and responsive. The technical details of the interference theory are less important for the teacher than perceiving the instructional implications of its two major manifestations: interference from prior and subsequent learning.

The interfering effects of prior learning are called *proactive interference* and can be symbolically-represented as: $A \rightarrow B \rightarrow b$, in which A is the prior learning, B the new topic being learned, and b the recall of this new B material. Reading the treatment in this chapter is itself an example of proactive interference if the reader holds preconception A about forgetting, which is at variance with what is being said here about B, and if, a month from now, the reader must take an examination b based on this chapter. This phenomenon is ubiquitous because students always bring prior learning to bear for understanding a new body of knowledge; confusion between the old and the new is inevitable later when recall is in order. The aim of good instruction is therefore more than just to teach the new B material; the better goal is to maximize performance in the b setting—recall on the final exam or later.

Debunking is a good example of a teacher doing something about proactive interference. Students come to introductory psychology, and to many other social science, science, and humanities courses, with some rather strong preconceptions about course topics, and the teacher tries to straighten things out, that is, to replace the prior A beliefs with a different set of B beliefs (Champagne, Klopfer, and Gunstone, 1982). Yet, even after a fifty-minute, B-purpose lecture, the conversion may not be complete. Directly or indirectly, the A beliefs intrude in one way or another, and this mixed-up state of information will show up as poor retention at the time of the final b examination. Effective debunking, therefore, is to help students replace "bad" habits of thinking—the facts and ideas they are accustomed to using—with a better set of information for storage in long-term memory.

Proactive interference is more pervasive in its effect than was first realized. No one is exempt, and it is a frequent source of trouble (confusion and resistance) in adult education. The memories of significant prior events in the lives of older learners influence how they perceptually filter and encode the new material and thus influence their retention and recall of the "contradictory" information now being studied. Verbal habits, mental sets, attitudes, values, and established beliefs stay in place as points of resistance and tend to interfere with the retention and recall of the "contrary" B material. Most students, of any age, defend what they already know and feel uncomfortable hearing (or reading) about how these prior opinions must be modified or even set aside. All of us tend to hang on to familiar meanings and feelings, and proactive interference will take its toll unless students understand and accept the logic and the data supporting the "new" ideas from the course. Otherwise, students will not really have reason to change their minds.

Interference by what comes after—paradigm $A \rightarrow B \rightarrow a$— is called *retroactive interference*. Note that here the interpolated B experience interferes with the recall of A when tested at a—rather than the $A \rightarrow B \rightarrow b$ condition in proactive interference. Retroactive interference is the classic paradigm in the design of experiments that questioned the disuse theory of forgetting. Interpolated learning at B results in lower recall scores at a than for a control group of learners for whom the B task is omitted, $A \rightarrow a$. Thus, one aspect of the folklore among students about cramming is soundly based: Cram, go to sleep, then get up and take the test; keep interference between study and testing to a minimum.

Within a given classroom, interpolated learning—the B factor—is built into the system as the teacher moves along from one topic to the next in advance of the midterm or final examination. In a well-organized course, the succession of topics combine into an integrated theme rather than "fighting" one another in some interfering way. The *similarity* of meaning between the A and B units is the key element determining the amount of interference. The instructional contribution is to make clear how the successive units are similar or different in meaning, how they supplement and support one another, or how they stand as relatively separate bodies of information. Forgetting through interference is, however, a reality, and the ongoing task of the teacher is to replace or counter these negative effects with rehearsal opportunities that will enhance the meaning of the sequence of topics.

A "Payoff" Schedule of Rehearsing. Figure 2 is an extension of the basic conception shown in Figure 1 (see Chapter One) and shows how rehearsal has the effect of changing the rapid forgetting of rote material to the long-term retention characteristic of meaningful ideas.

The fact that on Day 1 students reach a high point on the Y-axis in Figure 2 is no guarantee that the newly learned material will stay at that level. Forgetting is inevitable and the learner must keep on working. A full review of a topic on Day 2 should

Figure 2. Effects of Successive Rehearsals.

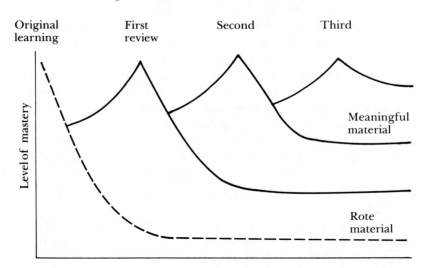

bring mastery back to par, and follow-up rehearsals—spaced over succeeding days—will again bring the information up to standard. The significant empirical finding to support this prescription is the *reduction in the slope of a forgetting curve following a period of rehearsal* (review, practice, coalescence, consolidation, elaboration). After a few such review sessions, the learner reaches a point where a quick glance at the major headings will bring back the essential meaning of the larger body of knowledge. A key word, symbol, or event is sufficient to remind the learner of the deeper meaning of the topic. The material has been transformed from the surface language of text and teacher into the language and images inherent to the student's own thinking and thus will more likely be retrieved in future settings.

A number of familiar instructional arrangements encourage students to rehearse and integrate course material: frequent testing, classroom questioning, spaced homework assignments, and study groups. The small discussion group is basically aimed at serving this purpose, and it is appropriate therefore to examine this instructional setting within the context of the present chapter.

Participation in a Discussion Group

A well-organized lecture is an efficient means for present-ing factual information, formal theories, and established pat-terns of knowledge and for enhancing the motivation to learn. The discussion group, on the other hand, is an excellent site for rehearsal, that is, for students to review textbook and lecture information, to explore and test the meaning of ideas, and to clarify for themselves certain value judgments, which might be derived from established knowledge (Webb, 1982). Students have a chance to practice making a point to their peers and to practice understanding what others have to say. These "practice effects" are valuable (see Chapter Seven), and just as writing helps to sharpen thinking, considerable truth lies behind the quip, "I don't know for sure what I am thinking until I hear myself say it." Budget pressures for large classes and the devel-opment of information processing technologies for self-study may reduce the powerful educational benefits of the small dis-cussion group.

Conducting an effective group discussion is a difficult form of teaching. In essence, the spotlight moves to the stu-dents as the teacher helps them review and extend the meaning of what was previously learned (Fuhrman and Grasha, 1983). These talk sessions range from "let's get acquainted" to the careful intellectual analysis expected in a graduate seminar. The literature is full of step-by-step guides for managing a group dis-cussion, but teachers will also benefit from understanding the group process, the dynamics of what is going on around them in interactions among students and between the teacher and stu-dents. The following analysis of these conditions is derived from a report by a career-long research specialist in group dynamics who, in this instance, was writing for his faculty colleagues—Alvin Zander (1979).

Reservation on the Part of Students. It is difficult for stu-dents to ignore the fact that the teacher is the authority who turns in the final grade, makes assignments, and may or may not write a letter of recommendation. Consequently, students speak in carefully guarded and tailored statements. If, to counter this reservation, the teacher proclaims the group discussion as being off-the-record so far as grading is concerned, students may downgrade the recitations as being superfluous to the serious business of educational achievement and decide that the situation does not demand one's best. This holding back about expressing oneself is made stronger if the teacher responds in a negative manner and without even trying to reflect the meaning or the feeling a student is attempting to express. It is easy to chill a student's interest about probing, out loud, the implications of an idea.

The teacher should develop the habit of posing questions for which there are no clearly right or wrong answers, for example, what was not clear about a presentation, what derivations follow, and the practical implications suggested by a body of information. When the discussion runs thin, it is time for the teacher to suggest a new idea or contrasting view about a topic and to encourage reactions revealing that there are no pat answers, that different beliefs are welcome in this forum. Silence is also welcome as offering a time for reflection (rehearsal), enabling all the participants to collect their thoughts without needing to listen to others.

A positive, reinforcing climate usually characterizes an effective discussion group. Students report that a cooperative inquiry is stimulating and refreshing in contrast to the rivalry and competition that prevail in most instructional settings. Two dozen students are about the limit for a productive discussion. Even so, teachers tend to talk more often than all the students put together. While teachers talk to the group as a whole, a student's comments are more likely addressed to the teacher than to the class, and we end up with a two-person chat. The instructional aim is to make varied ideas available for the group's consideration. Compiling a blackboard list helps to trigger ideas from the class as a basis for the critical discussion to follow. Such steps circumvent the pitfall of the unstructured bull session. A skilled discussion leader can prevent disjointed comments by requiring students to stick to the designated topic, to identify issues that merit attention. The expertise and perspective of the teacher are rarely a hindrance.

A discussion section is an excellent medium for rehearsal:

a time to pull bits and pieces together, to clarify the understanding of principles and procedures, and to gain some feeling of where this information lies on such value dimensions as trivial-significant, conservative-radical, and the like. The aim of a discussion group is to extend the meaning of information rather than to fix it in rote memory. Meaning is enhanced when students are able to merge what they have recently learned with values they hold. This merger is especially important for keeping knowledge in long-term memory and to elicit its retrieval later.

One of the best ways to learn something is to teach it—for the reason that the teacher is a thoroughly active participant in the presentation of carefully selected units of knowledge. Active participation, overlearning, and spaced rehearsal help to seal in the meaning of what was learned and, therefore, to sustain retention. Thus, good teachers provide the means by which students might review, reorganize, elaborate, and practice the integration of new information with what they already know. Forgetting, however, is an inevitable consequence of the interference from prior and subsequent learning. The teacher can reduce interference by enhancing the meaning students ascribe to the sequential topics of instruction. The discussion group is one opportunity to rehearse what one knows and to benefit from similar expressions from other students.

So much for "practice makes perfect." The substance of what is learned is the important thing for students to carry away. In my view, the concepts they comprehend and their ability to manage these ideas are the essence of quality education. We turn next to this important task of the teacher.

CHAPTER SIX

Guiding Students to Comprehend Concepts

The objective is to have students follow in some
sketchy but meaningful way the steps of a scientist. . . . Students will rarely come up with concepts
that are nearly as fruitful as those that the discipline has already developed, but at least they will
learn that concepts do not grow on trees, that they
are the products of much previous thought and research.   —Professor of sociology

Knowledge of things is not produced in us through
knowledge of signs, but through knowledge of
things more certain, namely, principles. . . . For
knowledge of principles produces in us knowledge
of conclusions; knowledge of signs does not.
    —Thomas Aquinas, *The Teacher*

The management of ideas is one aspect of thinking, and whatever else might be involved when students think, a teacher's satisfaction peaks when students show they can handle the impor-

tant ideas in a course of study. Comprehending and using concepts makes good use of their repertoire of cognitive skills: discriminating, remembering, imagining, inferring, creating, elaborating, reorganizing, generalizing, speculating, and abstracting.
Instruction taps these talents for thinking when abstract concepts
are derived from concrete events, when the past is projected into
the future, and when students are freed from the constraints of
time and place. Savoring the quality of a good idea beats wine
tasting any day, and the analysis of concepts of one sort or another dominates the curricular fare in higher education.

As the world of knowledge expands, but as years of formal education remain fixed, instruction selectively emphasizes
ideas that condense a domain of knowledge. Teachers come to
grips with how concepts are formed and how they are used; the
technological and social complexities of society require that students understand the conceptual world in which they will be living—and earning a living. Comprehending a concept is a moment
of instructional truth, and how well teachers, in all parts of the
college, direct this process is a fundamental measure of good
teaching.

Mathematics is almost entirely an abstract ordering of
concepts, as are advanced courses in the sciences. Insofar as the
substance of these offerings is linked to concrete problems, the
ethical implications must be addressed. The maze of human relations (the social sciences) is confusing when students fail to
appreciate the meaning of the conceptual aims and values that
guide the actions of people everywhere and at different times in
history. The conceptual language—trends, schools of thought,
and styles—in the humanities may be less formally structured,
but these value-linked ideas serve a vital integrating function.
Knowledge gained in the vocational and professional fields is
short-lived in the absence of understanding the conceptual context of specific procedures and empirical data.

The Catch-Up Between Research and Teaching

The science of psychology celebrated its centennial in
1979. Theories about human nature have changed over the
years, and methodological refinements about how the mind

works have moved this discipline toward a better understanding of the higher mental processes. To guard their status as members in good standing in the family of sciences, early experimenters searched out factors influencing overt performance (behavior) rather than trying to understand the covert, central processes of comprehension. Data and theories derived from the laboratory study of the conditioned response, for example, were more compatible with the rigor expected from a science than were speculations about mental states. This molecular fixation on behavioral analysis has changed with the more recent developments of cognitive science as an interdisciplinary effort among psychologists, linguists, philosophers, computer scientists, and educators.

As born-again scholars of the finer things the mind can do, cognitive theorists are reexamining the age-old question of how the mind works, how knowledge is acquired, stored in memory, and retrieved for purposes of understanding and solving problems. This research analysis is catching up with what teachers have been doing for a long time: directing the mental processes of students toward comprehending significant ideas. Current researchers speak of "ecological validity," meaning to take into account all the significant factors involved in perception and cognition. The aim of a good theory is to have "something to say about what people do in real, culturally significant situations. What it says must not be trivial, and it must make some kind of sense to the participants in these situations themselves" (Neisser, 1976, p. 3). Research today gives more attention to how students understand and remember connected discourse, that is, textbook prose, than to how they memorize (and forget) rote material.

These specialists use a particular terminology for communicating with one another, and some of their terms are becoming part of the instructional lingo of teachers: information processing, encoding, chunking, semantic memory, mental schema, retrieval, surface structure, deep structure, and cognitive maps. Many of these investigators are working both sides of the street—theory and practice—and by so doing are bringing research findings closer to what goes on in the schoolhouse (Glaser, 1973, 1982).

The Nature of Concept Learning

A formal concept is an idea represented by a name or symbol. Each discipline develops its special taxonomy of ideas, but, apart from these semantic differences, the *process of comprehending* what a concept means is a common-ground process for all disciplines. In essence, concept learning is recognizing the shared features of otherwise discrete events. What, for example, does the concept of "good students" represent by way of the linking attributes? Do these students have a certain grade-point average, attend chapel, behave politely to their superiors, achieve success after graduation? Agreement on the meaning of a concept is difficult without accepting particular common attributes, qualities, and features. In any field of study, the learner must be able to distinguish the common characteristics from an array of instances and to express these attributes in the form of an integrating rule or principle. Having made the integration, the student can then use this concept as the frame of reference for perceiving the meaning of new sets of separate events.

Relatively well-defined concepts such as income tax, sibling, and synapse are more easily understood than are the meanings of abstract ideas that mature through a lifetime—virtue, intelligence, and justice. Simple or complex, comprehending a concept is the means for making finer discriminations. Eskimos, skiers, and road crews use a rich conceptual language about snow just as politicians do about voters, economists about money, and physicists about atoms. These special groups use many words to describe qualities that are passed over by those whose language is confined to only a few classifying names. As our minds race along recalling past events, weighing alternatives, speculating about the future, and enjoying a fantasy, we find that ideas and images are more abundant than names and labels. Formal instruction about concepts, in comparison, moves in slow motion as teachers and students, at a deliberate pace, examine the process of comprehending a concept.

Perceiving and Abstracting. Verbal learning (memorizing) and conceptual learning involve different levels of intellectual processing. The nominal meanings of names and labels are relatively stable and are easily learned and tested. In contrast, the functional meaning of an abstract concept is more difficult to define and therefore to understand. The internal structure and the boundaries of abstract ideas are in constant revision as new data and events come to bear. The meaning of academic "competence" or "excellence" changes from one generation of students and teachers to the next. And so it is with the abstract concepts in the courses we teach—mental health, protective tariffs, carcinogens, physical fitness, and other concepts reflecting the findings from research and social changes.

In any case, and whether seeking to comprehend the meaning of a concrete or abstract concept, the learner scans the specifics in search of the general rule or generates a hypothesis, guess, or hunch, which is then tested against one instance after another. These strategies may be used in combination, but the result is an idea of categorizing and classifying (a mental schema) representing the common features in a sequence of perceived events. A concept starts out with a fuzzy meaning, but ends up as the tie that binds isolated perceptions into an integrated and therefore meaningful concept. For the beginning student, for example, "reinforcement" is first linked to pellet rewards earned by laboratory rats and pigeons, but further analysis and study extend this meaning to humans and to the powerful consequences of empathetic responses, affection, and love.

When a student finally comprehends the meaning of the internal structure and the boundary of a concept, some degree of freedom is achieved over the constraining influences of the immediate environment. The student carries in her own head the means to establish continuity, unity, and understanding from one item of experience to another; the concept user maintains an orientation in what might otherwise be a confusion of particulars.

Teachers sense the educational significance of the difference between memorizing specific information and forming abstract concepts; this distinction held my own research interest long before I became involved with research and consultation about the practical problems of college teaching. The basic contrast is learning to perceive (give meaning to) a particular item in the present environment versus learning to manage an abstracted relationship between two or more items or events. This fundamental distinction was clearly set forth in a research controversy that prevailed about thirty-five years ago: Do rats used in experiments learn to make a series of responses or do they acquire a "brain map" in learning to go to places? My own experiments with college students were tied to this question as students learned a sequence of twelve directional choices within a six-foot equilateral triangle. The *perception* (response) learners guided their back-and-forth movements via cues in the room containing the triangle while the *abstraction* (place) learners were blindfolded and learned to control their sequence of moves via a self-generated mental schema. The rate of original learning was about the same for both groups, but the abstraction learners were better able to carry the pattern of moves into a different room where both groups met the task of pressing a preset sequence of keys at the apexes of a nine-inch triangle. This basic advantage of the abstraction learners held true through various changes in experimental conditions (results published in Ericksen, 1962).

A follow-up study was one step closer to the natural setting in which students learn and think; the labels for the comparison groups were changed to *rote* and *concept* learners (Thune and Ericksen, 1960). Rote learners practiced the basic operations of adding, subtracting, and multiplying using a particular model of desk calculator. The concept learners practiced the same operations but, in contrast, were limited to using a schematic diagram of a calculator in general. The initial test of how well both groups learned was made under exactly the same conditions but using the particular calculator model already familiar to the rote learners. The slight advantage shown by this group disappeared on the tests of retention one week later. The most significant finding, however, was that the concept learners showed a 50 percent greater transfer advantage when tested with a different model of calculator. They conceptualized the essential features of calculator operation and carried this knowledge into the relatively novel testing situations.

These experiments underline the essential nature of concept learning: The brain extends what the senses bring in by forming a mental construct—a rule, principle, generalization, theme, idea, or schema—that reflects the common features in an otherwise variable scene or sequence of events. This ability to abstract allows the individual to move beyond the controlling influence of the immediate environment, and herein lies the advantage to a student preparing for the future. To paraphrase Kurt Lewin's cogent aphorism: Nothing is as practical as a good idea.

The Personal Meaning of a Concept. The words students read, the phrases they listen to, and the events they observe take on meaning in terms of what they already know. The learner *selectively* responds to incoming stimulation and gains understanding by reshaping the available repertoire of knowledge and values in memory store. Each person is an idiosyncratic individual and inevitably develops distinctive variations about what ideas mean; meaning always carries a unique quality even when answers are being given in terms of teacher and textbook criteria. This self-reference is illustrated by our use of a dictionary: We turn to this conceptual code book to confirm or to extend meanings already in our head. In the classroom, the teacher controls the general course of action by directing attention to a given topic, but each student thereafter learns and remembers the specifics in terms of his or her own processes of mental organization. In other words, the teacher decides what should be learned and monitors the private process by which each student gains meaning.

For reasons of economic necessity, students are grouped into classroom units, and they scramble to filter out whatever meaning they can get. Each student transforms what is given by the teacher, books, and other media into a cognitive structure generated by themselves. Since meaning resides exclusively and uniquely inside the head of the individual student, each is the unit of instruction.

Words and symbols may refer to a specific object—*Was ist das?*—or to a complex abstraction, validity. In either case, and literally in other words, each symbol or verbal chain is transformed into terms consistent with what each student is looking for and with what each already knows (semantic memory). A teacher of composition may, for example, set forth certain converging rules for good writing—principles experts stand by—but must be prepared to find students using all manner of diverging images, metaphors, and verbal nuances as each demonstrates a fluid meaning to otherwise stable principles of good writing, sound science, or reliable history. For the student, the process of studying is the process of reorganizing an internal, personal language in response to probes from the teacher, the prospect of a test, the need to solve a problem or write a sensible paper, or simply to satisfy curiosity.

Good teaching bears down on concepts as the means by which factual information takes on meaning, procedures are understood, theories are evaluated, values and points of view are judged, and applications are tested. Even so, most of the enduring ideas in a course are open ended; they allow some degree of distinctive interpretation. The constructs of a discipline mature and are reshaped as research and scholarship add new findings and conclusions. Likewise, students make finer discriminations about the meaning of a concept as they learn more about a subject. The teacher is mainly responsible for establishing the meaning of a concept within the discipline and confirming how well it is understood by each student.

Nevertheless, the balance between stability and fluidity of meaning is restrained when concepts are isolated from the reshaping influence of other courses, other teachers, and experiences outside of class. Variable encoding, that is, to examine a concept against different frames of reference, broadens the base of its meaning and its significance to the learner (Bjork, 1979). Further, an occasional reminder of the enlarged meaning of a concept helps to reestablish this idea in memory and to increase the likelihood of later retrieval.

Different Ways to Teach Concepts

Sooner or later it will be time to put this book aside and walk into the classroom. What happens then so far as teaching concepts is concerned? Instruction helps students learn the meaning of a concept by extending the study environment beyond the memorizing of names, dates, and factual data. Teachers often observe that students can express certain affective connotations of a concept—for instance, "civil rights"—but show only blurred understanding of the cognitive components. Students are talking in a vacuum when they use concept labels without comprehending the deeper meaning required to identify correctly whether a new instance stands within or outside the boundary of a given concept. Both positive and negative examples are important because some will confirm and others deny the validity of a given principle. Basically, this is what the Supreme Court does with its decisions about the applicability of a constitutional concept in a particular case. Negative instances may have the positive effect of helping the learner redraw conceptual boundaries and make them more distinct.

Many concepts have overlapping meaning, and it is necessary for the teacher to draw conceptual comparisons showing how, for example, vector is different from valence, correlation from causation, and simile from metaphor. Stanners and Brown (1982) analyzed the interrelationships among concepts in theories of personality and showed the pervasive nature of concept clustering in the minds of students. The more abstract the concept—dimensions of literature, characteristics of the scientific method, $E = mc^2$—the more difficult it is for the student to comprehend the boundary and the internal structure. Even so, as one instance after another is placed within or outside a conceptual frame of reference, the learner becomes more confident and even excited about being able to use ideas to establish continuity and meaning in otherwise variable events. A concept, like a melody, lingers on and can be recognized and appreciated despite differences in stimulus specifics.

The Lecture-Discussion Arrangement. Concept learning moves along faster when abstract ideas carry concrete labels. Science textbooks frequently designate such concepts by topical headings, and the teacher gives others—our lecture language is loaded with concept terms. Labeling is only the start, but it gives students a handle for holding onto a concept while searching and testing the relations between an instance and a rule, between an example and the principle. In an orderly and systematic manner, the lecturer directs attention to the atrributes pervading a succession of particulars that confirm (or deny) the relevant rule or principle. A guiding technique for concept teaching emerged during the early days of programmed learning: the RULEG principle—present the *rule,* the target concept, followed by *examples* given by the text, the teacher, or members of the class. This process continues until the teacher is satisfied the students can assess an array of additional examples as standing within or outside the rule, the concept under consideration.

In *Zen and the Art of Motorcycle Maintenance: An Inquiry into Values,* Persig (1974) steadily evolved the concept of quality from a set of attributes of a satisfactory term paper— "such as unity, vividness, authority, economy, sensitivity, clarity, emphasis, flow, suspense, brilliance, precision, proportion, depth and so on"—to the point where quality ended up as a philosophy of life. As faculty members, we debate the meaning of similar abstractions—the attributes of high academic standards, the limits of academic freedom, and the criteria for tenure. Fortunately, most of our instructional concepts are more easily defined.

Finding the best instructional balance between the particular and the general, between the example and the principle, is a recurring matter. Pitfalls stand at either end; factual recitals are impressive and empty rhetoric is easy to come by. To ask students to memorize a poem may be only the first step toward understanding the conceptual and affective meanings that might be derived from it. Preparing a reading log may indicate superficial awareness of the literature on a topic, but may not confirm that the student can expand on the deeper conceptual meaning of the cited items. Knowing a classification of mental illness says little about understanding concepts relating to the dynamics of the individual person. Solving a single problem in statistics is a weak guarantee that a student comprehends the principles involved.

Since the meaning of a new concept is influenced, if not determined, by the context within which it is presented, considerable classroom time is spent developing the background and the ramifications of a particular concept. This figure-ground relation is absolutely basic. When the teacher, for example, writes "π" on the board and asks its meaning, one student responds immediately with "3.1416," another says, "a Greek letter common in the names of fraternities and sororities," while a third student perceives this stimulus item as "part of an Oriental language—probably means a pagoda." Clearly, the meaning is derived from background factors pertaining to each student, and the teacher's task, therefore, is to develop a relevant conceptual frame of reference in a manner accessible to the students.

Students may nod their heads in agreement with the teacher, but the real test is their ability to verbalize the relation between an instance and the related concept, to link attributes with a relevant principle. When students give right answers but for the wrong reasons, we say they do not understand the integrating rule, the concept, pertinent to the situation. "Learning about concepts and learning to use an algorithm can be relatively separate domains of learning, and one or the other of these domains can be neglected by students because of the way instruction is organized and sequenced" (Greeno, 1973, p. 121).

The lecture-discussion is our usual mode for presenting and analyzing concepts, but several other instructional arrangements serving this purpose are considered in the following pages.

The Case Study. Several disciplines use the case method for concept learning. Law school students, for example, filter out the legal principles from assigned case studies that provide confirming or nonconfirming evidence of a given principle of law. A potential distraction is to become so involved with the details of a given case that the larger conceptual perspective is lost—or never gained.

The history of a good idea is a valuable resource for concept teaching. The longitudinal analysis of a complex concept involves its origin, traces its development, and clarifies its current meaning. What, for example, were the precursors to the concepts given by the First Amendment, how were they viewed in earlier years, and what have been the subsequent critical tests of their meaning? Teachers in science courses have access to fascinating research accounts showing the initiating idea for an investigation and how, step by step, the central concept became clarified to the point of its contemporary meaning. The pitfall in this approach is to gloss over the conceptual theme in the interest of telling a human-interest story and to ignore the fact that further revisions are inevitable as new data become available. The etiological analysis of an integrating concept is intellectually more demanding than the descriptive account of a sequence of events and settings.

Simulation. Simulation recreates critical decision-making situations and transforms abstract conceptions into concrete expressions. The fascinating history of training astronauts shows how simulation can anticipate a wide range of problems: from distinguishing "up" from "down" under zero-G to individual efficiency and crew interaction during long, intimate, and stressful periods of space travel. Simulation is an excellent test-tube arrangement for analyzing critical aspects of concept management.

For purposes of instruction, the teacher prepares a clear blueprint of the ideas to be carried from the simulation exercise to the real world. The aim is to help students make decisions and to understand events in subsequent settings quite different from the simulated setting. Rather than being passive observers, students exercise some degree of control over the sequence of events. The instructor must also be on guard that the procedural means of simulation do not become their own end. In the academic variations of *Monopoly,* for example, it is not whether you won or lost but why you played the game the way you did —understanding the internal conceptual links between decisions and consequences. A well-conceived simulation gives students direct practice in testing the meaning of a particular principle; it represents concepts in action.

Instructional Laboratories. Concepts relating to the methods of a discipline are often the most difficult to teach and to evaluate. For example, how well do students understand the rationale behind different types of experimental designs or the logic supporting the procedures in a scholarly analysis? It is not easy for students to recognize the limiting inferences from given sets of data, to note the actual or potential confounding variables, to provide a good operational definition for an inferential state, to appraise the limiting dimensions of a theory or scholarly synthesis, or to move from theory to application.

In the instructional laboratory, students simulate, in effect, the scientists in their efforts to understand procedural problems. They engage in a cognitive exercise to acquire technical skill and conceptual knowledge about research methodology, to define a problem, and to find out, firsthand, the procedures for gathering data that will confirm (or deny) the validity of the entering hypothesis. Filling in the blanks in a laboratory manual will not, by itself, accomplish these conceptual aims. The nature of the corrective action for laboratory instruction is a matter of debate. Some frequently used alternatives are: audiotutorial instruction, computer simulation, extending the boundaries of the laboratory to include off-campus settings and activities, and dropping the hands-on tradition in favor of a lecture-discussion course on, for example, the history of science. In any case, as teachers we still have a lot to learn about how to instruct students to be good solvers of problems within our own discipline, let alone how to think in the general case. Chapter Seven offers a few general guides along this line but, certainly, understanding the relevant concepts is prerequisite to successful problem solving in the laboratory or elsewhere.

Testing and Grading. Instruction is mostly via words, and some degree of mutual understanding between teacher and student must prevail about the meaning of the words, symbols, and labels used in lecturing, making assignments, and testing. Sensible students will anticipate and reflect a restricted set of conceptual meanings—those the teacher cares about—because the teacher sets the scoring key for objective examinations and evaluates papers and projects. Examinations geared to nominal meanings of factual information are quite different from those that evaluate the depth and quality of understanding a student has about the ideas themselves (see Chapter Nine). No apology need be made, however, for pressing students to know the names of anchoring concepts unless, of course, memorizing becomes a substitute for understanding.

It is difficult (but not impossible) to construct an objective exam to sample what each student knows about the limits and the internal composition of an abstract principle. Essay exams and term papers ordinarily give the teacher a better means to assess the quality of comprehension. Knowledgeable teachers will recognize the transient schemata students use as they seek to order different units of information. Students inevitably give different answers to the same question, but a competent teacher will be able to evaluate fairly the meaning expressed in the student's own words. While an instructor might be permissive with respect to how an idea is expressed, the evaluator must stand firm on the limits of substantive meaning given to the concepts being examined.

As it has been since Plato's time, the priority of instruction is to help students comprehend the meaning of ideas; this purpose plays to the strength of both teachers and students. In essence, concept learning is recognizing and comprehending a rule or principle for integrating a sequence of otherwise discrete items or events. Instruction is complicated by the fact that comprehension always carries an idiosyncratic quality; each student shapes the meaning of an idea against a distinctive, if not unique, personal store of knowledge. For purposes of instruction, conceptual material needs a label for students to use as they discuss these ideas. Concepts are fluid; their meaning changes as new information is gained and experience extended. Overt verbalizing about a concept is one thing, but its covert meaning is the active agent influencing how it is stored and retrieved later in different settings. Beyond lecturing, other instructional arrangements directly relate to concept learning: case-study analysis, simulation, and laboratory participation demonstrating how a discipline solves conceptual problems. Testing and grading amount to an operational definition of what the teacher holds to be the meaning of the concepts being examined.

Ideally, by the end of a course a student has weakened ties with the teacher and is prepared to move on alone by continuing to learn how to think independently—the most important single end product of education.

CHAPTER SEVEN

Teaching Students to Think Independently

> Probably the most violent and aggressive act that any person can do to other persons is to invade their minds with ideas and twists of meaning which disturb the comforting security of things known and faith kept. Yet this is what I, as a teacher, am required to do. —Professor of geography

> I won't teach a man who has no desire to learn, nor will I explain anything to a man who has no desire to seek his own explanation. —Confucius

College students have already learned how to learn but not as well as they might; this is one reason why their education continues. The prime responsibility of the teacher therefore is to help students advance from dependent memorizing to independent thinking and problem solving. This is the leading edge in educational reform, and this chapter examines how instruction can be stronger. Improved instruction is the heart of the matter,

the end for which curricular revisions, access to computer resources, merit pay, test-defined measures of student competence, and the many other reforms are supporting means.

The Science of Teaching and the Art of Learning

This heading reverses the title of B. F. Skinner's (1954)
classic article, "The Science of Learning and the Art of Teaching," but builds on his thesis: Good teaching is consistent with
certain general conditions for learning. My switch is intended to
clarify the role of the teacher as the person responsible for managing these conditions. As professional practitioners, physicians,
lawyers, social workers, therapists, and business managers transform general principles from their supporting sciences for
meeting the requirements of particular individuals. Teachers do
likewise, and the transition from the general to the specific is
neither simple nor straightforward; considerable skill is required
in guiding individual minds and motives in the study of particular units of knowledge.

As discipline specialists, teachers draw from an organized
body of information in marking out course content, but *instruction* in a classroom filled with individuals always requires that
addition, subtraction, and modifications be made to the supporting principles of learning—that is, motivation, rehearsal, and
feedback. The teacher is not likely to manage these changes effectively if he or she does not understand the depth and breadth
of these principles. The ways individuals learn to comprehend
must always be taken into account. The argument for the "art
of learning" applies to the student because the idiosyncratic expressions from the mind of the individual learner seem, to the
outside observer, to display the creative and unpredictable style
of an art form. Someday more will be known about "what goes
on in the Mind of the Learner" (Norman, 1980) but, in the
meantime, teachers must accept the fact that each student is the
unit of instruction.

Student-Based Factors in Learning. Good teaching trig-
gers the intellectual and motivational resources of each student.
A particular topic or style of teaching may be exciting to some

and boring to others, but the meaning gained from pages read, lectures heard, observations made in the laboratory or in the field, and actions taken in the clinic or studio derives from each student's distinctive meld of cognitive and affective capabilities (Hunt, 1983).

Early studies of classroom teaching compared gross features such as lecture versus discussion, the effect of a media presentation, class size, and the like. The usual finding of "no significant difference" is contrary to the very significant difference in the profile of achievement by individual students in a class. Critical factors were being passed over in studies based on average performance by the class as a whole. This oversight of individual differences is now being corrected by asking a thoroughly practical question: Which instructional method is best for whom? Studies of aptitude-treatment-interaction (ATI) analyze standard modes of teaching such as lectures, the media, and the Personalized System of Instruction as they interact with such aptitude differences in students as intelligence, anxiety, cognitive style, and personality characteristics (Cronbach and Snow, 1977). The findings of interactions are more statistical than "real" because they are based on measures of individual differences among large numbers of students. They are worth considering, however, since the involved administrators, teachers, and students seek the instructional advantages of grouping like-minded students (Snow and Peterson, 1980).

In his analysis of ATI, Tobias (1982, p. 5) cautioned that the mode of instruction and even the amount of time spent in study are secondary: "What counts is how the student uses that time and what the student is thinking while studying the material." He emphasized that the aim of instructional research is to assess the effects of such specific study activities as reviewing and rehearsing, summarizing and grouping what has been learned, recognizing points of limited understanding, and applying concepts and generalizations to specific instances; the level of comprehension and the relevance of feedback information are also assessed.

Teachers and students alike are sensitive to where they stand and how they are perceived on the dimension of "brightness"—a term with many meanings. In our academic subculture oriented toward aptitude tests, this measure is a prevailing index of "intelligence." Even so, it is a limited predictor of what it takes to do well in college. The correlation between Scholastic Aptitude Test scores and grade-point averages (GPAs) indicates that whatever this test measures accounts for no more than about 25 percent of the total variance making up the accumulation of grades. What student-based factors contribute the remaining 75 percent?

Motivation is prerequisite for learning, and if valid measures of motivation were available, they would probably correlate with GPA as well as do IQ-type scores. In either case—intelligence or motivation—the correlation is (or would be) low because college students represent a restricted range on both dimensions. Most are somewhere in the top half of the general distribution of intelligence and are also usually self-selected in terms of wanting to go to college. Many students do, of course, enroll in college for reasons tangential to learning substantive information; their motivation is inappropriate and their cognitive skills lie dormant.

In addition to intelligence and motivation, two large clusters of other student-based factors should be taken into account because they make a difference wherever and whatever students study: background preparation and personal characteristics.

High schools differ widely in the preparation they give students for college work. The informational prerequisites are deficient, and many entering freshmen simply do not know how to study; they have never engaged in the hard mental effort required to extract information from the printed page, to solve a set of homework problems, to write a paper, or to execute a special project. College study requires the ability to comprehend the printed word and to express ideas verbally and in writing. Remedial instruction, or its euphemism "developmental education," is part of nearly every college.

Most students hold positive attitudes toward their courses and teachers, but some have a chip on their shoulder. Negative attitudes make a real difference in what students learn and carry away from the classroom. The shy-assertive dimension is another personality factor in achievement. The instructional climate of classes, large or small, is tinged by an array of personal qualities in the form of interests, sensitivities, values, and aspirations that lead students to respond in a particular way to what the teacher says and does.

Students Always Learn Independently. The analysis of teaching is shortsighted when looked at only from the stimulus side, that is, the up-front presentation of information to a class. On the other side of the lectern, the process of comprehension moves along in a distinctive way for every student. Each individual listens selectively, encodes information in various ways, generates private elaborations of meaning, and remembers what he or she understands. Help from the teacher comes mainly from setting forth what should be learned, generating and sustaining motivation, and guiding study efforts along productive lines. Large lecture halls may be an economic necessity, but, at best, they implement a trickle-down pedagogical philosophy in which some students benefit but some are passed over. In a technical sense, teachers are members of an individual service profession; for example, they are required to report a course grade showing the performance of each student. This one-to-one responsibility is seen on every hand: acting as a mentor, counseling, and directing independent reading and special projects. In recent years a number of formal arrangements for individualized instruction have been developed. One of these is examined here, primarily to highlight certain important factors that support learning how to learn—a prerequisite for thinking.

Formal Arrangements for Individual Instruction

An analysis of the Personalized System of Instruction (PSI) is especially productive for extracting information about those particular conditions that promote and sustain learning by the individual wherever and whenever the student is working under the guidance of a teacher.

Self-Paced Supervised Study. Within the framework of lockstep progression through the succession of school grades, various adjustments are made to individual differences: grouping students by ability, honors programs, advanced placement, tutorial instruction, and independent study, for example. More recently the electronic and behavioral technologies have been used in developing various systems of individualized instruction: programmed learning, audiovisual instruction, computer-assisted instruction, and the Personalized System of Instruction (PSI). Keller (in Dessler, 1972), the originator of PSI, offers an impressive statement about the distinctive quality of this new mode of adapting instruction to the individual student: "In our educational institutions, it will involve less emphasis on rigid requirements and more attention to the individual, greater opportunity for success but with nothing provided gratis, more privacy for the person and less invidious comparison with others, less competition and more cooperation with others, and a greater respect for human dignity than has ever been shown before in large-scale education."

These expressions characterize the ideal college classroom, and it is appropriate therefore to examine those features of PSI—the Keller plan—that are designed to lead to this optimal educational setting. Three features stand out as factors that can be incorporated into conventional instructional arrangements to provide special support for learning by the individual student.

1. Mastery of sequentially organized units of study—in conventional teaching, we usually measure how much students learn within a given period of time, for example, at midterms and finals. In PSI, students demonstrate mastery of each unit before moving on to the next. This rigorous standard requires the teacher to be explicit about the sequence of study units and their criteria of mastery. Working out the details of such a course is far more difficult for the teacher than covering the field, but individual achievement will nearly always be enhanced when the teacher clarifies the subgoals of a course and requires preset levels of progress.

2. Individual rates of learning—the concept of self-pacing is powerful in its simplicity: The student is in control and moves forward or restudies whatever chapter, page, or exercise that seems difficult or is confusing. Some students need more

time than the usual academic schedule provides for working toward a performance criterion. Speed of learning is not a particularly valid measure of how well a student is learning.

3. Frequent and positive feedback to students—the proctor reviews strong and weak points with a student immediately after the mastery test is taken. This rehearsal helps to clear up ambiguities interfering with understanding, and a cooperative climate emerges because the students are competing against standards set by the teacher rather than against one another. This positive attitude counters or reduces the contaminating effects of anxieties, frustrations, fears, and confusions that so often degrade the atmosphere of the conventional classroom. It is surprising how much students can learn when they know what is expected of them and are supported in the achievement of these goals rather than threatened.

Research Evaluation of Individualized Instruction. One study rarely changes the course of pedagogical events, but a consistent trend of research findings might. James Kulik (1983), my colleague at the Center for Research on Learning and Teaching, was impressed by the steady stream of positive findings from PSI and other forms of individualized instruction; he made a careful analysis of courses taught conventionally versus those taught by PSI. In fifty-seven of sixty-one studies, final examination performance was superior in the PSI sections compared to those taught via the lecture method—an impressive finding. Further, student ratings of the value of the course were nearly always higher for PSI courses. From eight available studies, the superiority of PSI over conventional instruction was especially clear on measures of retention and the transfer effects to other courses.

The general pattern of positive research findings carries a message for every teacher interested in adapting instruction to help students learn how to learn independently. The three key factors just mentioned are certainly not patented by PSI, and in most courses good teachers can implement these conditions as a means of helping students to learn how to learn independently.

Practice Effects in Learning How to Learn

Learning how to learn starts before schooling begins, and preparation for college begins in homes where children learn that it is important to ask and to answer questions. In their classrooms, teachers continue to exercise intellectual curiosity and complain about the lack of such effort from teachers at earlier levels. High school teachers would like their students to come with better preparation in knowing how to learn; college instructors fault high school teachers for the same shortcomings, and professors at graduate and professional schools speak likewise. Pecking orders have a way of shaping up throughout society, and this instance simply confirms the pervasive nature of learning how to learn.

College teachers facilitate the linkage with high schools when they specify, in some detail, the prerequisite competence necessary for satisfactory performance in the courses they teach. Having this information, high school teachers can direct the study effort of their students toward these standards. Preparing students for the next level of education amounts to practice and rehearsal of particular skills and bodies of information. Students must read something and keep on reading if they expect to improve their ability to read. They must write something and continue to write if they expect to improve their ability to write. They must repeatedly solve problems in geometry and algebra if they expect to gain competence in these abilities as preparation for college work in mathematics.

These powerful practice effects continue through the college years. Seniors are considerably more efficient as students than they were four years and many courses ago; they have learned how to manage personal freedom, schedule and balance work and play, "read" professors, take exams, write papers, and give oral reports. Progress toward intellectual maturity is evidenced by their improved ability to define a problem, identify its relevant factors, and sense the limits of a generalization. After graduation, these finer discriminations are seen as "wisdom."

Carryover Effects of Practice. Instructional attention is

usually given to specific topics, but the nonspecific, learning-how-to-learn capabilities accumulate just the same. These dual effects can be seen, up close, in learning a second language. Initially, the prior habits of reading and speaking the first language seem to interfere with learning the new rules of grammar, vocabulary, and pronunciation. The specific negative elements are more than counterbalanced, however, by improvement in the general, nonspecific aspects of learning how to learn a second language. This general practice effect of learning how to learn does not have quite the same flavor as "disciplining the mind," but it comes close. Sooner or later, even laboratory rats seem to acquire and manage behavioral rules, for example, "don't re-trace because the food lies somewhere ahead." Monkeys are quite proficient in acquiring relevant "principles" for discrimination tasks: "To get the reward, always select (or ignore) the odd item from the set of choices in front of me." Humans, of course, comprehend such abstract concepts much faster—but they still need practice.

In the classroom or at the study desk, practice effects accumulate. History students, for example, get good at developing mnemonic schemes for linking names, dates, and events relating to history. Experienced actors display remarkable skill in memorizing the lines for a new play; they have learned how to learn this type of material but may be no better with names and dates than the rest of us. "When I learn the name of a student, I forget the name of a fish." This quip by biologist David Starr Jordan is delightful, but simply is not true. Memory does not perform a balancing act, but only reflects what was once learned.

Self-Selected Learning. In addition to learning what will be "covered on the next test," students generate useful schemes for organizing knowledge in their own heads. Individual interests, aptitudes, and cognitive styles come into play as they develop these cohesive mental constructs. Students follow self-selected paths of intellectual effort to establish meaning. This line of analysis may involve concrete or abstract ideas, revolve around words or numbers, express descriptive or analytical approaches, show a preference for visual imagery or conceptual references, use preset taxonomic grouping, or open up creative imagination. By various means, these mental schemata come into play. Students gain confidence in their ability to learn how to learn and to think independently as they write term papers, work through sets of problems, carry out special projects, compile reading logs, lead a discussion, and take different kinds of tests. These are the sorts of studying activities around which the practice effects accumulate, especially when students are learning what they want to know. Apathy, indifference, boredom, and negative attitudes will almost guarantee that learning, if any, has been teacher dependent and superficial, soon to evaporate. Learning in response to externally imposed pressures, or to reduce threat, fear, and other forms of "punishment," is equally transient—not always, but the probabilities are high. A positive motivational state is more likely to sustain self-directed learning over the years because it is guided by the curiosity to answer questions posed by oneself.

Independently Solving Problems

Parents are a child's first teachers about problem solving, and the process continues through the school years—and thereafter. College seniors are better problem solvers than they were in high school, and some part of this improvement can be credited to their teachers. In the classroom a teacher may take the high road: "The study of this subject will strengthen your ability to think and to solve problems wherever you go." Others take the low road with their well-placed purpose, "to teach my students how to think and to solve problems in the manner of an engineer (or nurse, biologist, or art historian)." Even so, this latter aim is a difficult and challenging instructional goal, and teachers face the temptation of overextending discipline-bound sets of problem-solving procedures. I taught experimental psychology for many years and too often drifted into talking about the worldwide value of the problem-solving concepts and methods of my discipline. Students soon realized that these sermonettes would not be covered on the next exam and quit thinking about how experimental psychologists solve problems. Restraint does not mean that a teacher should mute enthusiasm for a subject-matter specialty, but missionary work is not the same as instruction in the here-and-now complexities of problem solving within a given field of knowledge.

The problem for the teacher is to know how to guide students to understand the problem-solving process within a discipline and also to acquire some sophistication about the problem-solving process in general. As indicated in the preceding section, general and specific practice effects occur as students integrate, combine, and elaborate ideas from one course to others and to off-campus settings. The teacher can facilitate these extensions by use of appropriate examples showing the generality of certain problem-solving procedures. Students usually need help in learning how to identify and define a problem, distinguish inductive from deductive logic, discriminate direct from inferential data, and separate prejudgments from data. Many other refinements are needed for understanding the complexities of solving the kind of problems indigenous to every subject within the university (Reif and Heller, 1982).

Perceiving the reality of a problem means that something is missing—a relevant fund of information, an idea, or a skill, for example. Normally, our repertoire of verbal chains, conceptual pigeonholes, procedural habits, and value stereotypes are sufficient to take us around and over most conflicts and obstacles. One of the frequent surprises to students in a course is the revelation of problems that heretofore had been neatly closed by their preformed beliefs. This proactive interference (see Chapter Five) must be taken into account in the early stages of instruction about problem solving. In fact, the teacher might show how discipline specialists themselves marshal and realign theories, concepts, data, and procedures as they attack persistent problems (Champagne, Klopfer, and Gunstone, 1982).

It is vital for students to know something about a field before engaging in the heuristic scramble for solutions to its problems. Specific instruction about problem solving therefore should be delayed until later in the term, if not to advanced courses. When appropriate, the three following instructional principles have general applicability.

1. A background of relevant information is prerequisite to successful intellectual problem solving. Too much of the earlier literature on problem solving has treated this process as a procedural technique that can be gained by solving puzzles, playing intellectual games, practicing extensive drills, and learning algorithmic rules. Advocates here and there notwithstanding, no one has yet come up with a particular procedural technique that will, flat out, train the mind to be successful across the problem-solving waterfront. Problems exist everywhere; they are so persistent that people are tempted to spend good money for bad advice about how to become a better solver of problems. Quackery abounds. Teachers are sensitive to the fact that heuristic searching is less successful in an informational vacuum, in a mind void of pertinent knowledge. Investigators specializing in research on problem solving have found that the advantage of expert problem solvers over novices is mainly that they know more to begin with; they already have an extensive inventory of information from which to draw (Larkin, Heller, and Greeno, 1980).

2. Assuming that the teacher has taught pertinent information, the actual process of searching for solutions to problems gets under way. An effective problem solver usually demonstrates a variable attack by shifting the problem elements within a conceptual frame of reference or introducing a different context. This approach helps find the hidden relations necessary for a solution. A successful humorist also finds new and unusual relations, and our response, "Why didn't I think of that?," simply indicates that we were outguessed; we took a too rigid set toward an item and its context. The difficulties we have in day-by-day problem solving are, more often than not, the consequence of our holding on to a rigid perceptual or conceptual set—we perceive a newspaper only as something to read or to use for packing dishes but not for _____. Academia treasures diversity as a prerequisite condition for finding solutions to problems, and this principle applies with equal force in the trial-and-error engagement by the individual problem solver. A laboratory rat with a cortical lesion is inflexible and stereotyped in its efforts to solve a problem, and this same handicap is evi-

denced by a political leader whose needle is stuck on military solutions to problems. A variable approach is universal in its application to problem solving.

3. The ability to verbalize the steps taken in problem-solving strategies clarifies the critical components in the problem. A common example: A student approaches the teacher to talk about a problem, and he soon says, "I've got it"—before even finishing his statement about the quandary. Overt rehearsal helps the student to know what he or she is thinking about and to see conceptual relations otherwise blurred. The classroom lecture provides background information and guides about different problem-solving strategies but, sooner or later, each student must—with "hands on" or with "mouth open"—actively try to solve problems. In doing this, they reorganize what they know in searching for alternative relations; they direct their thinking along lines not heretofore familiar and move beyond habitual modes of analysis and synthesis. Clarification and restatement of the problem are, in themselves, key steps; in the hard sciences, for example, looking for qualitative relations may be the precursor to the final quantitative solution. Active participation and variable rehearsal are just as important for problem solving as for learning in general.

The current literature on the educational applications of research on problem solving is worth watching, especially those reports germane to a teacher's area of instruction. Considerable attention is being given these days to better teaching in mathematics and the sciences. The emphasis on problem solving in these fields is an appropriate outlet for the findings by cognitive scientists (Resnick, 1983). A conference on the educational applications of research on problem solving (Tuma and Reif, 1980) confirmed the complexity of such instruction and the importance of prior knowledge and procedural strategies. The field of engineering education is a source of useful information on problem solving, which has long been an active topic of discussion and instruction. Engineers have one marked advantage: The problem-solving variables involved in placing a man on the moon, running a space shuttle, developing solar energy, or finding out what to do about acid rain are more stable and controllable than are the ways of understanding and managing interest rates, world hunger, international peace, or even effective teaching.

Progress in learning how to learn independently occurs whenever students engage in processing information. The meaning of what they read, hear, and see derives from each student's distinctive meld of cognitive and affective experiences. In this sense, learning is an art while the teacher is a scientist directing student-based resources of intelligence, motivation, study habits, and personality characteristics. In recent years, formal classroom arrangements of individualized instruction (for example, PSI) have demonstrated three particularly effective means for enhancing independent learning that can be generalized to conventional courses: mastery of well-defined units of information, adapting to individual rates of learning, and frequent positive feedback to students. In the lifelong process of learning how to learn independently, two main features persist: giving meaning to specific items of information and the more general skills of learning how to learn. Problem solving is the essence of learning how to think independently, but students can only think for themselves. Efforts to find solutions to problems require a relevant fund of knowledge, diversity of attack, and an overt, active search for relations between means and ends. By encouraging such diversity and pressing students to acquire open attitudes and beliefs, a teacher is helping students to sustain independent intellectual inquiry and thereby to become somewhat a gadfly within a chosen field of study or in an otherwise complacent society.

This whole matter of independent learning frequently becomes stressful and generates the need for advice, counsel, and friendly support—the theme of the following chapter.

CHAPTER EIGHT

Teacher as Counselor and Mentor

Liking students, respecting them, deriving enjoyment from teaching them was the first of my cardinal rules for good teaching.
　　　　　　　　　　　　—Professor of economics

Socrates: Well, my art of midwifery is in most respects like theirs; but differs in that . . . I look after their souls when they are in labor, and not after their bodies.　　　　　　　—Plato, *Theaetetus*

The teacher is not a therapist and the classroom is not a clinic, but turning to the teacher is an early option when a student wonders what went wrong and what to do about it. Teachers appreciate the anxieties, confusions, conflicts, and tensions generated in the academic pressure chamber and are useful sources of information about course routes and career alternatives. Students seek out their teachers as persons whose judgment is respected and whose confidence is trusted as counselor, mentor, and friend.

The Teacher as Counselor and Adviser

On occasion, nearly every student looks for counsel about what is first and second and third on a scale of values. Conversations that penetrate (or skim) personal turmoils have always been part of the academic scene, and professionally staffed counseling centers are well established on most campuses. Learning how to handle worries and frustration is part of a student's education and, short of therapeutic intervention, teachers are helpful in guiding students through their personal curriculum.

Successful counseling amounts to an honest and friendly interchange of opinions and feelings—cognition and motivation again. Certain safeguards are in order because a student's self-esteem is too precious to be casually managed, manipulated, or massaged. In the role of counselor, the teacher is going beyond knowledge of his subject specialty and will benefit from observations by those more experienced in understanding the dynamics of an individual seeking help and support. Therapeutic specialists usually affirm that an empathetic attitude is basic:

> Good counseling . . . is reflected in the counselor's respect for the student's individuality, his special needs, and his right to accept or reject the information, advice, or assistance being offered. It rests in the counselor's ability to refrain from pushing the student into a preconceived mold or plan of action. It rests in the sensitivity that stems from being tuned in to the feelings and concerns often underlying the student's words and ideas. Such feelings as boredom, concern, anxiety, fear, and sadness are often revealed through subtle voice qualities, postures, and movements. Above all, good counseling is depending on the counselor's ability to enjoy and care for the students coming to him" [Bordin, 1969, p. 6].

Prior to entering this intimate relationship, certain practical considerations must be taken into account. Clearly, effective counseling is difficult when the teacher is the person who defines what the student is expected to learn and who evaluates the level of achievement. Nevertheless, the first concern is the well-being of the student as a self-sufficient individual rather than as a competitor for grades. This distinction is a categorical imperative. A second consideration is to recognize that symptoms may not be what they seem. It is precarious to project our own thoughts and feelings into the personal dynamics of someone leaning on us. Experienced counselors guard against such intrusion, and it is wise to refer a thoroughly alienated, frustrated, or emotionally distraught student to a counseling center or a health clinic to talk with a professional specialist. The following quotation is taken from a report by such a person commenting to his faculty colleagues about a teacher's responsibility as a counselor. Korn (1981) is the director of counseling services for the University of Michigan's Office of Student Services.

> There must be mutual understanding that the individuals involved have a right and an obligation to define the limits of the relationships. Both persons must have the sense of freedom to say "that's enough, thank you." It is unfair, and antithetical to promoting individuality, to encourage a student to expect something in a relationship which cannot be delivered because of limitations of time, role, or competence. I am describing a rather delicate balance which encourages a sense of trust on one hand and is explicit about limits on the other hand.

> Most students can make some kind of initial statement of what they are looking for, but where the student seems confused, frightened, or inarticulate, it is necessary to reassure this person that you recognize his or her conflicting state of mind.

> The attitude being suggested here is one of actively listening. This has a rather special meaning because it is one of the best ways for obtaining a

sense of the uniqueness of the other person. It involves the formulation of tentative hypotheses about what is important to the other person and about the major premises of the individual's belief system. The essence of this approach is to generate a hypothesis and test it out. For example, in response to a student's statement of the problem, you might say:

- You seem upset.
- Getting a good grade must be very important to you.
- Not knowing what you want to major in can be disturbing.
- Being bored could make you feel out of place.

In each of these examples the intent of the response is twofold: (1) to determine if your perception of the student's experience is accurate; (2) to focus attention on the student's need to further explore the significance of what he or she is explaining (to help articulate awareness).

Another dimension of this exploration phase is to determine how the student is conceptualizing problems. One must tentatively explore the student's beliefs about who, what, and why:

(a) Does the student need information about a course, an academic program, a possible career?

(b) Does the student need an opportunity to explore new ideas and their relationship to firmly established prior beliefs?

(c) Is there a need to talk openly about boredom and lack of motivation?

(d) Does the student need a chance to sort out major confusions about himself or herself or about a relationship with someone else?

At the same time you are deciding on any combination of these or other problems, it is necessary to decide who is the appropriate person to take the next step with the student. If you and the

student are interested, you may arrange more time
for dialogue. The more difficult circumstances occur when you are not interested, perhaps due to
time constraints or the feeling that you cannot
help the student. Making a smooth referral once
again requires careful attention to individual differences. Some students recognize and appreciate the
complexity of the university and thus are happy to
be informed about other sources of help on campus. Others are suspicious, resentful, or afraid to
approach somebody else with a problem or question. It is necessary to acknowledge whatever the
student is feeling and then to be clear and firm
about the desirability of the student seeking out
further assistance. This requires that you be informed about other sources of help and that you
indicate to the student that you would like to
know if the referral was helpful [Korn, 1981,
p. 5].

Academic advising, like counseling, considers students
one by one. The exchange of information dominates these conversations, but matters of motivation and aspirations are very
much in the picture. The aim is to help an individual plan and
carry out a course of study appropriate to a particular pattern
of interests, abilities, and ambitions. Teachers make good advisers because they understand the curricular complexities en
route to graduation or in preparation for postgraduate work.
Academic advising requires homework to know the intricacies
of intra- and interdepartmental rules and regulations and to
recognize and relate different courses to a student's future. The
advisory relationship matches the resources and requirements of
the school with the resources and the aims of the individual student. The director of the University of Michigan's advisement
program in the liberal arts college pointed to certain considerations about advising:

Advisers need to encourage students to think
about why they are in school. In this sense, the ad-

viser is an educator. Too many students select courses term after term without questioning or thinking more broadly about what they might obtain from their education. A few perceptive questions or insightful comments can cause students to rethink their goals. . . . The successful academic adviser offers students a feeling of personal concern within the institution, provides accurate information—which often includes referrals to other campus agencies—and attempts to help students discover the best possible fit of their aspirations with the values of a liberal education [Judge, 1981, p. 6].

Mentor to Students

Certain groups of students are clustered for special attention. Of these, honors students are the favored group for mentors' attention; they learn quickly, ask challenging questions, and reflect faculty values. It is rewarding to support these students because it has long been observed that any instructional program involving bright and motivated students is doomed to succeed. This section, however, will examine acting as a mentor to those students who have problems in the classroom, those who have not yet acquired the motivation or the techniques for comprehending quickly what textbooks and teachers have to say.

Most schools are taking steps to adapt instruction more effectively for the underprepared student. As Cross (1982–1983, p. 1) stated so well, "There is no equality until each student is offered the right to do his or her best. Sad to say, we have not been offering that right to either high-achieving or low-achieving students. . . . I am convinced that we can return pride in achievement to education without compromising the gains that we have made with respect to (equal) access. But to do so will require major changes in the traditional practices of education—changes in our most basic premises about teaching and learning." The mentor's effort is directed to factors that can be changed, such as motivation and study skills. Slow students have not had especially pleasant experiences with formal education and face the frustration of, once again, not doing as well as they would like. Discouragement comes quickly, and they need mentors who can counter defensive maneuvering, a lack of interest, self-defeating attitudes, and the weak study habits acquired in earlier school years. Few college teachers have had experiences corresponding to those of a student coming in for help and worried about not being able to make it. Being a successful mentor for such students requires, as does counseling, empathy and understanding of the dominant role of affective factors in a student's schoolwork.

Student Underachievers. The academic performance of some students is noticeably below what might be expected in light of their scholastic aptitude scores or earlier achievements in high school. The freshman year is often a difficult time for students unaccustomed to high performance demands. For reasons other than lack of aptitude or not knowing how to study, they have trouble with core curricular subjects such as mathematics or with the foreign language requirement. Instruction may be satisfactory, but it falls on deaf ears—motivation is weak. Variations of the boredom theme are frequently expressed. Classes limited to technical procedures, specific applications, or taxonomic ordering are, to some students, less stimulating than courses immersed in theory, conceptual analysis, problem solving, and the value implications of issues that have challenged the best minds in history. The values of a liberal education do not always sing out by themselves, and the social, educational, and professional values of the teacher-mentor influence the student's course of action. Motivational redirection is accomplished by both precept and example.

Variations of the following question are heard over and over again when teachers talk about classroom problems: "How do I motivate the bottom third of my class?" In this instance, the motivation factor may be overextended because the trouble may be inadequate sets of study skills.

Basic Skills for Study. The first diagnostic appraisal following admission to college should be for competence in reading. Even fairly good readers find their skill inadequate when faced with the unrelenting pressures of long reading assignments. Poor reading is an obvious handicap that can catalyze, if not ensure, academic failure. Slow readers cannot move freely among words seeking the thread of an idea. Increasing speed, however, is not equivalent to increasing comprehension, although it may lead in that direction. Good measures of reading skill are available, and there are few excuses for starting students through a reading-dominated curriculum without making the effort to correct reading deficiencies.

In the late 1930s, many American colleges and universities established remedial reading programs for their students. Broader supporting services were eventually developed as faculties realized the importance of the larger set of study skills. Successful work as a college student requires a complex meld, a combination of reading with writing, writing with thinking, taking notes from lectures and from reference materials, preparing for exams, planning and writing term papers, solving sets of problems, carrying out special projects, and scheduling time for study and for play. In advising or instructing students along these lines, one must give careful attention to motivation because the lack of sustained interest is the most common single reason for failure to complete a study-skills program. Fortunately, the confidence gained by students who see improvement in their study habits enhances their motivation and thus their perseverance. Participation in a study-skills program is an example of a justified self-fulfilling effort.

The ability to express oneself with the written word—to describe events and to analyze abstract relationships—is a distinctive and valued talent. Writing a book report, or poetry, and everything in between can be improved with supervised practice, and colleges are finding that "Freshman English 101" is not enough for many students. Comprehensive programs of diagnosis, training, and evaluation are being developed to improve the ability of students to write (Bergman, Rubenstein, and Dunn, 1982). A number of schools are implementing a new academic requirement: The writing competence of each student is certified by teachers in, for example, an advanced course in a student's area of concentration. Learning how to write requires practice in writing about whatever variety of things students study in their courses. Insofar as they are qualified to do so, teachers in all departments should assume more responsibility for the quality of written discourse. This added dimension to the instructional task may call for institutional support plus more extensive research analyses of the basic skill of writing (Frase, 1982). Consultation, workshops, and printed information might examine appropriate kinds of writing assignments and how to intervene as an evaluator of a paper's organization and style. It is appropriate, for example, that students write papers aimed at an audience beyond the academic setting, for example, chemistry for cooks, history for voters, and manuals for new owners of home computers.

For better or for worse, and for both teacher and student, performance on examinations is the dominant measure of a student's academic competence. The following chapter examines testing as a measure of good teaching, but the matter is here considered one of the basic study skills. When studying for an examination, the student is trying to anticipate the mental gymnastics of the teacher searching for good questions and framing the answers. Students should have an opportunity to "practice under game conditions" by taking what might be called "instructional quizzes."

These tests are not entered into the student's record, but are used as an instructional guide. In large classes where objective exams are used, the teacher might start a class hour with a multiple-choice quiz of five items. The answers are self-scored and a show of hands will probably indicate that most of the students made the right choice on most items. This immediately tells the entire class that neither the teacher nor the test was a culprit; the test questions are fair and valid. More important, the teacher can show how the questions sample the substantive material to be covered on the next formal examination. A few such rehearsals will link the testing thinking of students with the teacher's approach; anxiety is reduced and the students have learned about how to prepare for the midterm or final examinations. Their study skills have been strengthened. Similar procedures can be followed in providing practice for essay tests. The extra work required of the teacher is a legitimate demand considering the importance given to grading.

Friendly Instructional Relations. Inside or outside the classroom, teachers make good friends for students interested in getting the most out of college. It is easy to be friendly to bright students who emulate the teacher, but the demand for this friendly understanding and acceptance exceeds the supply for nontraditional students. What support can teachers give those students who stand on the fringe of the traditional social mechanisms that developed to serve the interests of young, robust, white, middle-class men (and some women)? A few institutional adaptations to the new students are under way: ramps for the handicapped, service and support units for minorities, and tuition and schedule adjustments for part-time adult students. Considerably more action by the faculty is necessary to remove nontraditional students from shadowed standing as second-class scholars.

Since this book is about instruction, my analysis of the teacher as a friend will stay in the classroom to show how the demographic attributes of these new students can be used as a resource for better teaching. My particular vehicle for this analysis is the adult student participating in a formal course of study. This rapidly expanding group of college students illustrates well how a teacher respects the sensitivities of students and builds instruction on what each student has to offer. A patronizing attitude is, of course, inexcusable, and this is why particular attention is given to certain guiding principles for managing the classroom hour rather than to personal interchanges between teacher and student.

Specialists in adult education perform a valued service in making clear the social and institutional changes needed to encourage and support lifelong learning (Wolfgang and Dowling, 1981). For the classroom teacher, however, only a few instructional habits may need to be modified. These considerations derive from two basic characteristics of the adult learner: motivation and memory.

Most older students are paying a personal price to go

back to school and are alert to the relations between means (instruction) and ends (course objectives). Consequently, they expect the teacher to stick to the subject and to demonstrate that it is worth knowing. No special motivational padding is called for if the teacher does, in fact, have confidence in the educational benefits of the course content. Learning is just as satisfying for the older students as it is for their younger classmates. At the start, older students are self-conscious about being "different." Their self-esteem is on trial, and they present a well-rehearsed list of reasons why they may not keep pace. These stereotyped beliefs about "rusty brains" should be countered by making it clear that presumed age-linked factors have little basis for support. The need to strengthen one's habits of study is not limited to those who have lived a little longer.

It is pedagogically overreacting to tailor a course tightly to the inferred motivational characteristics of a particular group of students—older, handicapped, from other countries, or in a minority classification. Illustrative examples might be used in line with the expressed interests of such students, but the value of a course will be attenuated if the content is consistently modified for a particular category of students.

All students, young and old, must learn to manage their study in an environment of potential distractions. The adult student may not have more conflicts than younger students have, but they are likely to be different—family responsibilities, pressures from a full- or part-time job, and commitments within the local community. A friendly teacher will recognize a circumstance that is adverse to study and, within limits of fair play to other students, make appropriate adjustments. Another, but persistent, source of interference is internal: the conflicts derived from memory.

Over the years, adult students have accumulated a rich variety of significant experiences that have helped to mold their beliefs and to shape particular habits of thinking. On occasion, these prior values and opinions seem to clash with what the teacher has to say—especially in the social sciences and humanities. "If what the teacher says is right, then my beliefs, attitudes, and ideas are wrong," and few students accept such contradictions with alacrity. Defenses begin to appear when cherished ideas are, in effect, being debunked by the textbook or teacher. Whenever these barriers crop up, they interfere with both learning and retention. This state of affairs is a direct classroom example of the proactive interference paradigm $(A \rightarrow B \rightarrow b)$ described in Chapter Five.

The teacher can and should take steps to minimize the confusion between prior learning and the kinds of responses expected, for example, on the next test. Experienced teachers can anticipate likely contradictions as perceived by students and deal with them openly and with due regard to the sensitivities of those whose ideas must change. The instructional problem is complicated by the dynamics of memory. Students may, on the surface, understand and accept a new line of thinking but, as time passes, their prior motives and values reenter the cognitive picture to reshape and sustain the older beliefs, which then interfere with the clean retention and recall of the new meanings.

Cognitive interference is simply one example of a teacher's instructional considerations for adapting to the special characteristics of a particular group of students—in this instance, the adult learner. Students from foreign countries frequently need guidance and practice in learning how to study for and to take machine-scorable examinations, compile a reading log, write term papers, and so forth. (I once had a transfer student from the Orient who had never taken an essay exam and, in the same class, a student from an African country who had never taken an objective examination.) Minority students often report feelings of social isolation; they have a limited identification with the traditions and aims of the institution and the larger body of students. Conflicts and confusions are ubiquitous; some are tangential, but others are significant intrusions to effective work as a student. Each student is different, and friendly teachers are sensitive to these differences and do what they can to reduce interference to academic success.

The guiding principle for the teacher as a counselor, mentor, or friend in the classroom is to respect and respond to the individuality of each student. A sympathetic ear is prerequisite to effective counseling. Rather than a teacher running the risk of unwittingly influencing decisions having long-lasting consequences, thoroughly confused or fearful and distraught students should be referred to a person or unit offering specialized assistance. The academic adviser brings educational realities to the student's attention, and this includes both information and motivational support. A mentor works with those students who need special attention in meeting the goals for graduation, strengthening the basic skills for college-level study—for example, reading, writing, and taking tests. The demographic factors relating to any student can, in the hands of a friendly teacher, be used as a resource rather than as a barrier for productive instruction.

One technical task of the teacher cannot be farmed out: evaluating student achievement with respect to what will be carried away from a course of study. We turn next to the significant issues of testing and grading.

CHAPTER NINE

Assessing the Achievement of Each Student

I consider examinations to be useful, both in providing students with feedback on how they are doing and in telling the instructor how he is doing, and I am not sure at this point which is the more valuable contribution.

—Professor of economics

Similarly, if you describe, commend, or expound a subject to another person, you will never be sure whether he has grasped it, though you repeat yourself a thousand times; but you will quickly make sure, if you question and examine him to test the degree of his comprehension.

—Comenius, *Special Methods*

Faculty standards for A-grade performance express, significantly, the academic values of an institution. Rhetoric aside, the transcript of credits and grades is one concrete way of stating what each student has accomplished by way of classroom learn-

ing. A teacher's authority reaches its peak—but not its fulfill-
ment—with the assignment of a grade.

The use of tests for selection, placement, and systemwide
standards of competency is a controversial matter that lies beyond the scope of the present treatment, which examines the
means for assessing students in a particular course of study.
Evaluative judgments start with decisions about who is admitted
to the school and end with status designations of honors and
prizes at the time of graduation. In between, teachers are con-
stantly discriminating good, better, and best, and this responsibility cannot be set aside. The instructional and evaluative use
of tests and other measures of achievement is central to the
teacher's task. The opening paragraph of Rowntree's (1977, p.
1) insightful book states the educational reality, "If we wish to
discover the truth about an educational system, we must look
into its assessment procedures. . . . The spirit and style of student assessment defines the *de facto* curriculum."

Evaluation Is More than Grading

Grading is an administrative shorthand for classifying students and reporting their levels of accomplishment as they move
through the curriculum. It is a system for placing students in
categories prescribed by the institution, and the grade-point
average (GPA) has become an important basis for special
awards, admission to advanced training, ego enhancement, and
employment prospects. With such payoff potential, it is self-
defeating for a student to be indifferent toward grades or for a
teacher to be casual or careless in assigning this index of competence. Most students are motivated by these public signs of
achievement, and grades do influence how hard they study.

Grading is an end-product measure, but evaluation is ever
present and is indispensable for learning. Evaluation is a direct
link between cognition and motivation because students want
to know if what they know is correct or incorrect. As they move
into unknown intellectual territory, students must have guide-
posts to confirm that they are moving in the right direction. The
return of evaluative information comes from several sources:

qualitative responses by the teacher to specific examination questions, marginal comments on a term paper, and a conversation with a student. Evaluative cues are given by the teacher's tone of voice, facial expressions, and silence—the absence of confirming signals. Students derive further evaluative information when talking with classmates. The most persistent and available form of evaluation, however, comes from a student's own feeling of understanding the material at hand (see Chapter Four).

The traditional convention of grading has become a type of academic currency important for the interchange between schools and the larger community. The information given to a student by way of a grade is too gross, however, and comes too late to have a constructive influence on here-and-now learning. Grading has to do with housekeeping, evaluation has to do with learning, and for learning, grading is ridiculous, evaluation is sublime. The confusion between grading and evaluation reaches ironic proportions at a typical honors day convocation. Here certain alumni may be recognized for their distinctive accomplishments as individual citizens, scholars, or professionals. The undergraduates, on the other hand, are rewarded for their skill in maintaining a high GPA: the 3.80s and above get blue ribbons; the 3.79s and below go unnoticed. The alumni are evaluated in terms of the quality of what they have done; the students are graded along a quantitative scale. In the administrative shuffle to sort out these students, the criteria for the quality of performance are irretrievably lost. The distinction between grading and evaluation stands out when we examine how tests can be used as an instructional aid.

The Instructional Use of Tests. Frequent testing has certain advantages: It helps to sustain habits of study, it leads to a more reliable final grade, and it provides ample opportunity for the teacher to make qualitative evaluations of student performance. This close-up, evaluative analysis starts at the beginning of the term.

Diagnostic evaluation is not a covert operation, but is openly announced as a means for helping students gain maximum benefits from the study that lies ahead. Because prerequisite courses frequently fall short of their intended purpose, a series of diagnostic quizzes early in the term will inform both students and the teacher about topics needing special attention. When students realize the significance to themselves of diagnostic probing, they are more likely to open up and reveal low points in their preparation profile, anxieties, misconceptions, and deficiencies in knowing how to do certain tasks. Diagnostic information is useful in its own right, but this effort also tells students that their teacher seems to care about how they do and is taking concrete steps to help them along—an excellent attitudinal climate for starting the semester.

Superior test performance probably indicates that a student is well prepared, but a low test score needs further interpretation. Is weak performance due to the lack of information or is it confounded by distracting interests or low motivation? A thorough diagnostic appraisal may call for nontest inquiries about background factors such as an appraisal of earlier courses, the possibility of negative attitudes toward course-related conditions, false expectations, or an overloaded schedule of work, study, and play.

A low total test score may signal the need to study harder, but the appraisal of specific test responses is instructionally more significant than knowing the total test score. Correct answers to questions are, presumably, worth knowing; further analysis is called for when incorrect responses are given to particular test items. When a student says, "I still don't see why the question was keyed that way," the inquiry is started toward unscrambling the false connections. In this close-up look, the teacher may note a pattern of mistakes showing the lack of understanding of a particular rule, procedure, or principle; on the other hand, some students have the right answer for the wrong reason.

If a large number of students are stumped by a question, the phrasing of the question may need clarification, and discussing this weakness will help to straighten things out. If several answers were possible, examining the alternatives will increase the students' understanding of the distinctions among the different items. Reexamining answers to questions serves as a review or rehearsal session for the information to be remembered.

Instructional quizzes have the advantage of helping students learn how the teacher selects questions and keys their answers. Because the total test score is ignored, attention is focused on specific questions and answers, on information rather than on grade scaling. A frequent sprinkling of short, diagnostic quizzes early in the term is especially helpful for confused and slow students.

Students study most in preparation for a test, and they structure this effort around their expectations of how they will be examined. If they anticipate the need to know unassimilated facts, they will memorize; if they expect to be required to integrate, extend, and evaluate, they will study toward these ends. Thus, frequent testing and other feedback arrangements serve as progress reports about the course. If students' expectations are at variance with those of the teacher, they can make the correction before it's too late.

Some encouraging things happen when students realize the instructional advantages of taking a test and reviewing the profile of findings. A sort of intellectual x ray shows what they know and how well they are learning. This benefit is, pure and simple, a demonstration of the power of feedback—reinforcement, knowledge of results, confirming information—as the necessary evaluating mechanism for self-monitoring the progress of learning.

Contracts for Learning. Ordinarily, test results are used to stretch a class along a scale where cutoff lines are drawn between the A's and the B's, the B's and the C's, and so on. The teacher controls the test-sampling exercise of what students know. One distraught student expressed her antagonism thus: "I just don't like to play the professor's game—'I've got a secret, see if you can guess what it is.' " Those who correctly anticipate what the teacher wants them to know receive good grades.

An alternative route—contract grading—has merit because the grading standards are openly set in the beginning. A negotiated learning contract between teacher and student makes the individual student the active agent for achieving self-selected goals within the boundaries of the course. The competitive agitation among students is ruled out, and the guessing game between teacher and student is replaced with a joint commitment about what is to be accomplished. The contract may allow for demonstrating achievement by any number of means, separately or in combination: objective tests, a reading log, problem sets, short and long papers, special projects, oral exams, and other mastery criteria deemed relevant by the teacher.

Contract teaching does not take the instructor off the grading hook; the vital margin of quality of achievement must be evaluated. An insecure teacher may lean on the quantity of work as an escape mechanism for buffering the usual confrontation with students about grading. A teacher should seek confirmation from department colleagues about the criteria for a contract plan. Peer review about the inner mechanisms and goals of one's course is not a common practice, but is good protection in case the final grade distribution gets out of whack. Which it may, since it is surprising how many students opt for and achieve the A-contract when they know what they are expected to accomplish.

The Teacher-Made Test

Exam week is not the happiest time of the year as students cram and cut corners to earn high grades. They start to learn the subtleties of test taking early in their school careers— to study, for example, in line with what they expect of a particular kind of test: multiple choice, true-false, short answer, or essay. Despite polite phrases about "learning for learning's sake," students are aware that courses mean tests, tests mean grades, and grades mean the difference between success and failure. An examination is also a revealing comment by teachers about what is important in a course and how achievement in these topics is fairly measured. The quality of a teacher's procedures for testing and grading should carry substantial weight when peers judge the competence of a teacher.

In a grade-oriented academic society, much of the total instructional process hinges on testing and grading. And yet, compared to familiar topics of using technological aids, group discussion, and teaching style, relatively sparse analytical attention is given in the literature to the critical matter of the valid assessment of student achievement. The recent analysis by Frederiksen (1984) makes clear the instructional strengths and weaknesses of both professional- and teacher-made tests. Of particular significance is the distinction between the "well-structured" test problems characteristic of standardized tests and the kind of test problems a teacher could generate to test the carry-over effects of instruction to "ill-structured" problems encountered after the course is over. A faculty seminar on college teaching could, in fact, be organized around the logic and procedures for testing and grading. The discussion would bring out the interlock among (1) course objectives—what should students know by the time they take the final examination? (2) the management of the classroom hour—does the teacher talk about what testing is about? and (3) methods for evaluating student performance—are they fair measures of educationally worthwhile goals? *The integration of these three components is basic to good teaching.*

The technology of testing is highly refined, but this section is hardly a manual on how to do it. I will, however, review some procedural concepts that promote fair and discriminating testing. For the most part, teachers teach better than they test, partly because testing is an extremely complicated procedure involving both scientific and ethical considerations (Messick, 1981).

Machine-Scorable Examinations. The construction of objective tests demands time and talent. It also demands money in those instances when external exams are purchased from professional test makers. Psychometric specialists can prepare tests at the appropriate level of difficulty and discriminating power, but they need careful briefing and close editorial monitoring to ensure that the tests reflect the goals of the course and the material emphasized by the teacher. *Validity* is the prime criterion of a test since it is unfair to interpret a test score as a measure of what a student has learned about a subject when it actually measures something else, for example, an index of reading ability or of general intelligence. In principle, teachers should construct their own examinations while having, nonetheless, ready access to technical assistance from specialists in the local testing bureau.

Reliability—internal consistency—is the second standard of a good test. A rubbery yardstick is probably the most common weakness of teacher-made tests. The most straightforward solution to this problem is simply to increase the number of items in the test as a means of counterbalancing the random errors of interpretation and responding by students. When important assessment decisions must be made for large numbers of students, technical help will nearly always be in order—the development of a test-item bank, item analyses, assessment of the wording of questions, and the like. In any case, certain items in a test will turn out to be confusing to students and may even show a negative correlation with the total test score. These bad items should be eliminated before assigning the final examination grade.

To mislead, confuse, and use trick questions does nothing but reduce the reliability of the test and weaken confidence in the validity of the evaluating arrangement. In a negative climate, cheating is encouraged. Messick (1981) and Schrader (1980) offer excellent guides for the large domain of testing and grading; Milton and Edgerly (1976) consider the technical specifics of test construction. With respect to objective exams, some common pitfalls are the use of ambiguous words and phrases, negative (or even double-negative) statements, excess verbage, subtle but unintended clues to answers, and inappropriate level of difficulty—items that are too easy or too hard add little to the discriminating power of the test.

Testing and grading students is stressful work, and teachers are, understandably, inclined to be defensive and to stand firm behind the authority of their position. This stance is inexcusable if the testing instrument was badly made or if a good test was badly used. The technical aspects of assessing student achievement are probably the most vulnerable point in the overall competence of college teachers.

Students may complain about their score on an objective test and will fault particular items in the exam but, at least, the target of their criticism is the instrument rather than the interpretation and judgment by the evaluating teacher. This is not so, of course, with the essay exam.

The Essay Exam. If constructing an objective test is a dreary and time-consuming task, so is grading a stack of blue-book examinations. In the former, composing the questions is the hard job; in the latter, grading the answers is the chore. A machine-scorable exam tends to test recognition memory—the nominal, surface meaning of words and symbols. In contrast, the questions in an essay exam can be directly in line with the long-term objectives of the course as they probe the deep-structured meaning as encoded in the student's own words. The clarity of the questions is, of course, important, but accurate evaluation rests on how accurately the teacher-reader makes the diagnostic appraisal of the strong and weak points in the argument presented. It is possible, for instance, to note that a student is giving a good answer but to a question that was perceived somewhat differently than the teacher intended. The answer to an essay question is a miniature term paper expressing how a student has organized a meaningful unit of knowledge. The student's thinking is not being irrevocably forced into a standard template by a rigid scoring key, and this degree of intellectual freedom is necessary for the teacher to assess the potential long-term retention of the substance of instruction.

The mechanics of evaluating essay tests are simple:

1. Read one question through the entire set of books—the reader's initial expected answer is bound to change as he reads the variety of interpretations.
2. Scramble the stack of blue books—to balance the inevitable drift while plowing through one opinion after another toward favoring a particular pattern of answers.
3. Each exam booklet should be read "blind" with respect to the writer—to forestall confounding influences of personality; we do find some students to be more attractive than others.
4. Do not rush the returns—early return of information about test performance may be appreciated, but this business of immediate feedback is overdone. Students can quite easily

recreate their original test-taking thinking when reviewing the questions and answers one or two weeks later. The qualitative critique and evaluation by the teacher are worth waiting for.

Term Papers. To organize an integrated chain of thought, elaborate on findings, and communicate ideas to others is a stronger test of achievement than is the recognition or recall of isolated bits of information. A well-planned assignment of term papers is an excellent teacher-made test. I am partial to this measure of student achievement because it gives students a greater release to express their own thinking and is faithful therefore to the intellectual demands following graduation. The term paper is a reflection of what the individual student has learned and how all this information is pulled together for comprehension and understanding—which is necessary and sufficient to keep this knowledge available in long-term memory.

Given this special status, the teacher should prepare a handout setting forth the guides for preparing a paper: due date, length, use of references, and any restrictions about style and other mechanical aspects of the assignment. The major criteria to be considered in the evaluation should also be stated. Specifications differ from course to course, but, across the board, discriminating thinking and clear writing are essential in term papers. For example, is the student describing when analyzing would be a better approach? Are the student's own ideas hidden behind extensive references to textbook and teacher presentations? Marginal comments give the teacher's reaction to what the student is trying to say or did not say.

A term paper is an array of words to express certain important concepts or thematic ideas. The student's specific language may paraphrase these ideas but, in so doing, it represents the nature of the mental material that is likely to be part of the student's thinking for some time to come. The kind of information organized in a term paper is a fairly accurate measure of what a student "got out of a course" and what is packaged for carrying away. This type of evaluating assignment does not compromise the conditions for learning and retention *or* the grading demands of a school.

The hard work of grading a set of term papers is counterbalanced somewhat by the satisfaction of reading the better papers, and some of these are truly exciting. In fact, the reading experience is instructionally too valuable to be limited to the teacher alone. Consider using the "jury" procedure for making instructional use of term papers. Peek (1982) described an informal arrangement for the jury-graded evaluation of student themes in a freshman composition course. Department resistance led to its abandonment but not before it was demonstrated that the major goal could be achieved: "objective, accurate, and consistent evaluation of student performance on written themes" (p. 75).

My own practice was to arrange for each student to read from three to five papers and write "marginal comments" on a separate sheet of paper. Each paper, therefore, received independent evaluative comments from several peer readers. The reader's attention is limited to evaluation because the teacher is responsible for grading. Despite the sometimes logistical headaches, students report this jury arrangement to be very much worthwhile—both the giving and the receiving.

The Meaning of the Final Grade

Measurement requires a zero point, and two basic options are available for grading: (1) norms set by the range of student performance as they compete against one another on a statistically manipulated distribution or (2) teacher-defined criteria of achievement. Historically, the teacher's authority was unquestioned for making decisions about student achievement. The invention of the grading curve brought about significant changes; the reference standard shifted from the teacher's judgment to a grade defined by reference to the average performance of the class. The former was an *absolute* evaluation, the latter is *relative*; in the technical language, evaluation approaches involve criterion-referenced versus norm-referenced standards.

In practice, these two approaches overlap and merge. It is difficult, for instance, to read a set of blue-book examinations and not be influenced by the general level of student performance; teachers can hardly help but make evaluative judgments in terms of the levels of accomplishment with which they are accustomed. The faculty at even the highly selective institutions see the bottom quartile of students as being "rather uninspiring and intellectually weak." In any case, teachers are still in a controlling position as they define course objectives, prepare the examinations, and decide on the cut-off points between grades.

Grades influence what happens to students all along the educational ladder: their selection for specialty high schools, college, graduate programs, professional schools, and honors and prizes. One would think that the cumulative assessment of over two dozen different undergraduate teachers would be a solid index of a student's ability to acquire knowledge in general, to solve problems, and to cope with intellectual matters in many different settings. The GPA, however, is a weak predictor of performance later on (Sampson and others, 1984). Why?

For one thing, the graduating seniors walking across the platform to receive their diplomas are a relatively homogeneous lot so far as grade-related skills are concerned—those whose interests lie elsewhere are elsewhere. Those present have learned how to cope with the intellectual demands of the college classroom: They are fairly good readers and note takers at lectures; they have learned how to study for tests, to write textbook-like term papers, and to complete academic special projects. Their GPAs are a composite index of these skills for success as an undergraduate student. Advanced work continues many of these study habits, but some variations occur. In professional and graduate schools, considerably more weight is given to the ability to transform general principles into application and to plan and carry out independently conceived research projects. Phi Beta Kappa graduates generally do well wherever they go, but in the past, many stayed in academia and made tenure for demonstrating almost exactly the same talents that earned them a place in the honor society in the first place.

The predictive power of grades for off-campus endeavors drops even farther. Chickering (1983) reviewed such research findings about post-college performance but was particularly concerned about how the mishmash of an accumulated GPA could possibly predict career success. Success as a practicing lawyer, physician, businessperson, or civil servant is only indirectly related to factors leading to success as an undergraduate student. For one thing, the weight given to personal qualities increases: tolerance for stress, risk taking, ambition, love of money and other material status symbols, conformity, independent decision making, and the need to be liked, for example. Having the right connections also helps—and so it goes. It would be nice if the GPA were a measure of the ability to sustain congenial human relations, to assume responsibilities, and to cope with and to solve unexpected problems, but it simply is not. A teacher's letter of recommendation might help to fill in the gaps but, here again, opinions differ and such endorsements have a low predictive value.

Higher education has acquired a strong dependency on grades as a medium of information exchange and will not quickly forsake this currency. The grades we give are based on student responses to information and values emphasized in our courses. These standards serve the academic purpose, but it is precarious to generalize the meaning of grades beyond the quality of achievement within a given domain of knowledge: what students know and what they can demonstrate by taking formal tests and writing papers on topics and in the style prescribed by the teacher. If others feel the need to extend this meaning as a predictor of general intellectual and personal aptitudes for meeting demands in settings outside the classroom, that is up to them.

This extension of grades from gown to town is related to the competency issue being reviewed at all levels of formal education. Test makers are having a field day as school systems set minimum test-taking performance standards for graduation to the next level of schooling, or for a specific basic skill, or to be certified as a teacher, and so forth. The objective is worthwhile but the debate brings forth two basic issues: (1) Is a machine-scorable test a valid screening device? Does it measure what students were actually taught in their classrooms? (2) To what extent are teachers accountable for the demonstrated level of test-taking performance?

Teachers are paid to move students along the learning curve, but they do not, of course, exercise control over all the significant variables that influence learning. Further, in mass-testing arrangements, students are measured against standards laid down by others; the minimum becomes the norm and individuality is curtailed. Teachers quite rightly resist the containment that judgments about competence be made in terms of what can most easily be measured. Higher education is an open system of intellectual inquiry, and college teachers hesitate to penalize the diversity with which students examine and acquire knowledge. It is painful to teach for a test measuring the ability to answer minor questions, to demonstrate specific skills with nuts and bolts rather than the creative and imaginative use of ideas to solve problems.

One accommodation has been to use the narrative system of reporting student achievement: Conventional five-point grading is set aside, and the instructor writes a qualitative statement describing the distinctive proficiencies and achievements demonstrated by each student. The pass-fail and the credit-no credit methods of grading are, in theory, less pressureful than conventional grading and are, therefore, appropriate for first-term students. At the other extreme, where prescribed standards of competence are well established—as in a professional school—there may be less pressure to squeeze students into discrete places on a quantitative grading continuum.

As God looks down on Ann Arbor (or any other college town), He or She sees more sin in the category of testing and grading than in classroom teaching. Reform and repentence in these matters will have been made if teachers:

1. Use testing as a diagnostic means for evaluating where students stand when the course gets under way and to follow up with constructive remedial action when such is indicated.
2. Provide frequent opportunities for students to receive evaluative confirmation (feedback) of their progress on each important unit of study.
3. Assign a valid grade—one that is consistent with the actual course objectives and standards of mastery defined by the teacher.

Grading contracts are worth considering but, for the most part, grades will continue to be based on teacher-made tests, essay exams, and term papers. Each of these has particular advantages for grading as well as for instruction. A high grade is personally rewarding, and students work hard for grades and accept the realities of the competition and the importance given to these external signs of success; the universal equation of grades and excellence does not escape them. Individual teachers must guard the criteria of performance set for the students because everyone pays the price for academic inflation when these standards are lowered.

The valid and discriminating evaluative judgments we make of our students are also what we should expect from our students and from our peers when they are asked to evaluate our teaching.

CHAPTER TEN

Evaluating the Quality of Instruction

Not one word spoke he more than was his need;
And that was said in fullest reverence
And short and quick and full of high good sense.
Pregnant of moral virtue was his speech;
And gladly would he learn and gladly teach.
    —Chaucer, *Canterbury Tales*

The resistance of teachers to evaluation is not to defend a criterion-free work place, but they do want an appraisal to take into account the distinctive qualities emerging from their interaction with peers and with students, and the situation-specific demands of a particular subject. Variable starting points are the rule; for example, one student writes, "This teacher is just what I have been waiting for," while, in the same class, another will say, "Please replace the professor." Judgments of a given teacher by administrators and faculty colleagues often show the same extremes. The merger of many yardsticks is needed to measure teaching: student ratings, student achievement, peer review, judgment by supervisors, and the teacher's own appraisal of the quality of the work being done. "None has features sufficient to recommend it alone. Furthermore, reliance on several information sources, with the kaleidoscopic patterns and contradictions that they will reveal, provides a valuable reminder that the arts of effective teaching are too numerous, varied, and subtle to be accounted for fully, much less simply" (Seibert, 1979, p. 71).

Crosscurrents in the Evaluation of Teachers

A narrowly based evaluation system can penalize the inventive or unconventional teacher by giving higher rewards to those who conform to preestablished norms about teaching. Instructional diversity is a resource to be enhanced, not washed out. Since the time of Socrates, great teachers have held true to their distinctive selves. College faculties cherish the freedom for individual expression and guard any compromise raised by institutional procedures for evaluating how they teach. Mainstream descriptors of teaching tend to float over the crosscurrents that put the individual teacher in a swirl.

The criteria for career success are not usually posted on a bulletin board or encoded in a set of bylaws, but, just the same, various dimensions of merit are in force at the local institution. These standards grow and take form as traditions develop and as changes occur in the academic setting. Some schools accept individuality more easily than do others, but it takes courage to march to a different beat than the one given by the dean, or the power structure within the department. The adaptive route is to note the totems and taboos in the administrative chain of command and to mold oneself into a favorable line of vision— to teach for the tests that apply. This conflict is a reality of institutional affairs, but is also an invitation for faculty leaders to press for instructional freedom and flexibility.

Another crosscurrent is between evaluation for administrative purposes—pay and promotion—and the diagnostic information one seeks for instructional self-improvement. Data that go forward through administrative channels for merit review serve quite a different purpose from that of information about how to strengthen one's impact on students. If a colleague visits a class for a diagnostic evaluation, are the results, in effect, being "taped" for later scrutiny by a review committee? This conflict is especially noticeable in the use of student ratings: Who sees the results and for what purpose? In the absence of trust, any evaluation scheme is doomed to flounder.

Fair play also requires that an evaluative distinction be made between the qualities of a course and the person in charge. By the very nature of their subjects, some courses disturb, frustrate, and threaten students while others are entertaining and stand clear of intellectual challenge. Substance and style are not, of course, completely independent; a dull teacher can destroy an otherwise exciting body of knowledge, and a charismatic teacher can breathe life into dreary textbook knowledge. Nevertheless, it is not uncommon for students to like the course better than they like the teacher, and these discriminations should not be obscured by the evaluation procedure.

The principle behind the aphorism "The power to test is the power to control the curriculum" applies with equal force to the evaluation of teachers. To what extent might a teacher mold classroom performance to coincide with the instructional styles and standards held by supervisors or faculty colleagues? When a central authority issues a standard scale for evaluating teaching, many instructors strain to receive high marks even though this paper routine may seem superficial, if not tangential, to a teacher's own way of doing things.

Student Ratings

Students have ringside seats to teaching, and their composite judgment has the special advantage given by the force of numbers. Combined observations have a degree of consistency that cannot be matched by a single opinion. The only serious question has to do with validity—the extent to which student judgments are, in fact, related to good teaching. (Validity is examined later in this chapter.) Students know some things about their teachers but not everything, and some aspects they observe are, to them, unimportant. Attention to housekeeping chores might, for example, be given weight by administrators and by peers, but whether or not the teacher carries out these logistical duties neatly and on time is of little consequence to students; their interests are linked to what goes on inside the classroom.

Information for Others. As a source of information, student ratings indicate to the larger body of students how a subgroup evaluates a particular course and its teacher. Students are curious to know something about an unknown teacher: the mechanics (procedures) of a course and whether the substance deviates from or holds true to the bulletin description. The two objects of their curiosity—teacher and course—are to some extent enlightened by the results of student ratings. These ratings indicate what students judge to be important, for example, instructional objectives, how class time is spent, flexibility with regard to student options for different activities within the course, use of supplemental resources, grading standards, frequency and nature of testing, and those idiosyncratic characteristics of the course and the teacher that count to some students. There is no serious question of validity here; if students want to know what other students think of a course, just ask them.

Student ratings often influence administrative decisions about salary increases, retention, and promotion. This raises the question about the career progress of a teacher being affected by anonymous evaluations. Unsigned criticism has little to do with accountability and violates the civil rights of the teacher as an academic citizen. The careful gathering of pooled opinion, however, is less subject to this criticism. Even so, if the teacher believes that student ratings do not give an accurate reflection of classroom performance, ample opportunity must be allowed for offering contrary information in defense of one's instructional competence.

Overall Ratings. The research analysis of literally hundreds of various rating forms indicates that most of the load is carried by two general items—one about the course, the other about the teacher. The instructor-designed questionnaire used at the University of Michigan (Kulik, 1976) includes two such items:

1. I would recommend this course to others.
2. I would recommend the instructor for this course to a fellow student.

Each rater marks one of five choices: strongly agree, agree, neutral, disagree, strongly disagree. The reaction to these two items carries the weight of the argument so far as an overall evaluation is concerned.

In addition to these two foundation statements, three other questions make up the core category of items on the University of Michigan questionnaire:

3. The instructor motivates me to do my best work.
4. I feel that I am performing up to my potential in this course.
5. I had a strong desire to take this course.

Item 5 offers a correction factor in terms of the initial motivation of students toward, for example, required versus elective courses. Adjustments like this one improve the worth of student evaluations by establishing more equitable reference points for making comparisons between teachers. Using statistical norms is a tricky business for something as diverse as college teaching. Student ratings should be compared only between teachers in reasonably similar situations: level of course, types of students and course (required or elective), and academic status of the comparison teachers. These background considerations are not, however, nearly as important as the factors relating to the individual teacher.

Caution is in order when interpreting the results of general, overall teacher ratings. Most students like their teachers and say so, and this "halo" effect shows up in the skewed distribution of ratings. Most scores are lumped toward the high end, and a composite rating of "average" probably means that, in the eyes of students, the teacher should make some changes in how the classroom hour is handled.

A second reservation has to do with decimal-point differences. A rating questionnaire is not a precise measuring instrument; except for large classes, minor variations in reactions to items and total scores can be ignored. Evaluative justice is strained when a peer-review committee compares a 4.35 on the course with a 4.16 on the teacher to mean that students like the course better than the teacher. Empirical indexes, for example, IQ, SAT scores, and GPA, have a way of becoming overinterpreted.

What action should be taken when the evidence persists on repeated ratings, and is confirmed by other sources, that a teacher is a weak instructor? The research findings (Cohen, 1982; Centra, 1979) show that consultation with a credible person—preferably, someone outside the home department—can lead to instructional improvements. The overall rating, however, is only the starting point; constructive action depends on having specific information about those aspects of teaching that need changing.

Diagnostic Information for the Teacher. Students see certain components of course instruction more intimately than anyone else, and their opinions have considerable value to a teacher. Particular benefit is gained when the teacher is free to select or construct questions directly pertinent to his or her own concerns about personal performance—"How am I doing?" In line with this desire to know, many institutions use an arrangement that allows the teacher to select questions from a large catalogue of items and, if desired, to add a certain number of items tailored to meet particular questions about one's own teaching. Narrative statements can also be introduced.

Given these options in the University of Michigan student-rating system, it was found that most teachers select items that refer directly to themselves—"the instructor"—as, for example:

- The instructor appears to have a thorough knowledge of the course.
- The instructor gives clear explanations.
- The instructor seems well prepared for class.

Less popular selections by teachers are items about what happens to the learning and motivation of students:

- I learned to apply principles from this course to new situations.
- I developed enthusiasm about the course material.
- I learned to value new viewpoints.

Teachers frequently want to know how different elements of the course are received: the textbook, use of other media, testing, physical conditions in the classroom, discussion sections, and the like. Items about these topics supply pertinent information, but rating scores are usually lower than for items directly related to the teacher; they are less subject to the "halo" effect. In any case, anonymous reactions to external questionnaire items are a distinct improvement over the practice in a former day of asking students to write, on the last page of their final examination, "your positive and negative reactions to this course."

Many departments, student organizations, and individual teachers construct evaluation questionnaires on their own. Unfortunately, these arrangements are subject to biased samples, inadequate conditions of administering the scale, vague or double-barreled items, and capricious norms. They fall short of the procedural standards needed to do justice to courses and teachers. Refinements resulting from consultation with a professional specialist in this area of research and development add credibility to the rating form itself, strengthen the procedures for its use, and clarify the interpretation of results. The evaluation of teachers is a sensitive issue—the flip side of complaints and defenses by students about grading—so the system of student ratings must be carefully monitored to keep it fair and up to date with respect to developments in assessment.

Research Findings About Student Ratings. The analysis of pooled student opinions is the subject of many independent studies. I will synthesize these data by casting them around the gist of questions frequently asked by subject-matter teachers.

Does the technical quality of professionally developed questionnaires produce results that can be trusted? The reliability coefficients are generally in the range of .75 and some attain the .90 level (Seibert, 1979; Overall and Marsh, 1982). This correlation range means that these instruments provide relatively stable data. Such consistency cannot be obtained without considerable pretesting of items, assigning scale values to response options, and specifying optimal conditions for administration.

To what extent do extraneous teaching conditions, such as class size and course level, influence student ratings? The research findings offer only weak support if one is looking for a scapegoat, for example, "You can expect only low ratings from an eight o'clock class." A teacher's reputation precedes and influences subsequent student ratings, and a senior professor starts out holding a slight advantage over the apprentice teacher. Marsh (1982) analyzed what is probably the most relevant single type of comparison, namely, changes in student ratings in the same course taught twice by the same instructor. Evaluations are usually slightly better for the second offering, but other background factors (student expectations, work demands) have little effect. Empirical findings, however, derived from correlations and statistical averages about these background factors have only passing interest to the individual teacher concerned about why one student likes what the teacher does but another dislikes it.

How valid are student ratings? The answer, of course, depends on the conceptual starting point, for example, popularity with students, respect among peers, standing in the eyes of the administration, one's private self-concept, or the most rigorous standard—What do students learn and carry away? It is hazardous to try to implement this latter standard because confounding variables make it difficult to pinpoint the specific influence of the teacher. A delayed examination of learning (retention) is rarely feasible and would, in any case, reflect the confounding effects of numerous intervening variables resulting from such additional external experiences as the influence of other courses, other students and teachers, and uneven access to supplementary resources. One direct approach to assessing the validity of student ratings is to compare the achievement of students working under different teachers in a multisectioned course. The influence of the different teachers approaches the status of an independent variable because several of the other significant factors in learning are relatively constant—the motivation to take the course, the textbook, and, in some instances, a course-wide system of testing and grading.

A practical question is frequently asked: Do student ratings help to improve instruction? The answer must be qualified by the kind of improvements that are needed. A low rating on a general item such as "I would recommend the instructor for this course to a fellow student" offers less diagnostic help than "The teacher mumbles and is hard to understand." Student appraisal of specific aspects of teaching amounts to a discriminating evaluation to which the teacher can respond in concrete ways. For purposes of self-improvement, however, it would seem almost mandatory that the instructor have some control of the questions asked students, to receive information relevant to the instructor's concerns about areas of strength and weakness in the classroom. Otherwise, students are telling the teacher more than he or she wants to know, and little change is likely to take place. Cohen (1980) showed that, in any event, constructive changes are more likely to occur with the help of an instructional consultant having access to the results of student evaluation.

Peer Review

Faculty members hesitate to intervene in the instructional affairs of their colleagues; peer review, therefore, is an acid test of the legitimacy of the collegial form of faculty governance. Schools differ widely in the extent to which the faculty is involved in decisions about pay, promotion, special honors, and appointments to key administrative positions. Of these, the tenure decision is the critical judgment—the moment of truth for evaluating and predicting how well the now-apprentice teacher will sustain professional competence over the long haul. At this point, the standards and the values of the department and the institution come into focus. A commitment is being made that this individual will be a helpful if not a congenial colleague, a productive scholar and researcher, and an effective teacher in the years ahead.

The security of tenure is not, of course, its own end but is the means to ensure open inquiry to wherever intellectual problems may lead. Academic freedom encourages individuality, diversity, and the expression of contrary opinions as immutable qualities of teachers who influence students. Faculty colleagues are more likely to perceive and to appreciate these values than are students, and their judgments preserve the vital distinction between popular teachers and those having a long-term impact on students for reasons other than their ability to entertain.

A peer review system must be carefully planned and executed to ensure fair play, to warrant the trust of one's colleagues, and to forestall the likely sources of discontent when negative conclusions are made about a given teacher. A pass-fail decision is being made that has momentous consequences to the candidates. However, such a decision is absolutely essential for preserving the quality of teaching and the high regard our society places on higher education.

For practical purposes of evaluation, a review committee usually considers the faculty role in three parts: research, teaching, and service—and probably in that order of significance. Teaching, however, includes more than classroom performance; it reflects the general reputation of the person under review. *Reputation* is a fuzzy word, and as Kulik and McKeachie (1975, p. 227) point out, "The prospect from above is not different than from alongside.... A teacher's reputation as 'good' or 'poor' may get started in student circles, but the grapevine stretches up as well as out and faculty members soon get the word about their colleagues." This is exactly why a peer review committee must extend its analysis beyond the more visible performance aspects of a teacher's contribution.

The candidate under review should offer the first body of evidence—a best-foot-forward argument for promotion. A review committee will normally seek supplementary data from department files, student ratings, local recommendations, and, perhaps, appraisals from external referees. The tenure decision requires the integration and synthesis of data about long-lasting aspects of a candidate's professional competence. As someone said, "Research counts because it can be counted," and this implies, true enough, that the quality of research and scholarly productivity is difficult to assess. Valid consensus judgments about the quality of a research publication—its impact within a discipline field—cannot be made quickly. Likewise, an evaluation of the long-term impact of a teacher requires longitudinal appraisal—from one year to the next.

In an excellent review of the literature on the role of colleagues in evaluating college teaching, Cohen and McKeachie (1980) made clear the importance of dimensions beyond those that might be rated by students. Colleagues are best qualified to evaluate critically significant factors, such as the following:

- Depth and breadth of knowledge related to what is being taught.
- Selection of course content and its organization.
- Appropriate use of resource materials—readings and audio-visual media, for example.
- Quality of student assessment—tests, papers, and projects.
- Teaching methods consistent with course substance.
- Commitment to teaching, to students, and to the instructional program of the department.

No one of these dimensions is easy to judge; they all require the careful analysis of extensive data and information from a variety of sources. The weight to be assigned to the different aspects of a teacher's job is a perpetual debate within a department and in the larger "labor-management" confrontations at the institutional level. An evaluative decision will, in many instances, be questioned, but the considered judgment from a group of peers is a valuable asset for appraising the career contribution of a member of the faculty. Good teaching is not something that can be taken for granted, and evaluative checks and balances will always be needed to guard the welfare of students, individual teachers, and the institution.

Self-Appraisal

Thoughts about content and process are on the mind of a teacher the year around; self-appraisal is continuous—before, during, and after class. We are our own best consultants for what to do when students send signals that a certain instructional unit is flagging, when we observe new techniques of instruction by peers, and when we appreciate the need for a different ordering of knowledge derived from research and scholarship in a field of specialization. Information that may lead to better teaching is gathered from a variety of sources: informal conversations, conferences, workshops, professional journals, magazines, and books. Some teachers proclaim the value of observing one's teaching self on videotape—a television replay. This is always an interesting but sometimes disturbing experience. In viewing a short sample, we find our attention riveted on mannerisms of which we might not have been aware—but to which students become accustomed since they observe us hour after hour throughout the term. Style of presentation is a packaging part of teaching, and we should look behind these behavioral techniques and appraise the substance of what we are talking about, how it is organized, the values we express, and the attitudes we reveal toward students and subject matter. Whatever the source—talking, reading, viewing—the suggestions, admonitions, and directives we receive are filtered through our own store of knowledge and the opinions we hold about the nature of good teaching.

Consistency is key to success as a teacher. The evaluating criteria imposed by the public, governing boards, administrative supervisors, parents, students, faculty colleagues, and associates in the discipline are relatively impersonal abstractions of "paper" teaching until theories are transformed into action via the distinctive qualities of the individual teacher. These self-sufficient persons provide the balance and the continuity that, week by week, sustain the integrity of the course. Students can adjust to all manner of different ways of teaching—from authoritative to permissive—if they know what to expect rather than if trying to anticipate what strange, stylistic maneuver might be placed before them.

Experienced teachers are not usually surprised at what is on student rating forms. They have traveled this route before and can discriminate short-term appeal from long-term educational benefits. If a student is less than excited about completing a particular assignment, the self-consistent teacher holds firm in knowing that this same student—as did his mother or father—will later come to appreciate the value of understanding such things. In the last analysis, we must place our evaluation faith in how the individual teacher feels about the value of what is being learned. Student ratings, peer review, and special awards are only a shadow of the intimate interaction between teacher and student and the self-esteem derived by both from that interaction.

Evaluating the quality of instruction is like trying to tame a bear while hanging onto the tail. We cannot do fancy tricks because the other people involved—teachers, administrators, and students—already have well-formed beliefs about good teaching. We cannot let go because accountability is intrinsic to professional responsibility. In summarizing his review of the research literature on student ratings, Seibert (1979, p. 18) observed that "the elusive coefficients which have played hide-and-seek with many investigators are one more indication that effective teaching . . . remains an inviting and worthy phenomenon to study, especially if one has stamina and a high tolerance for frustration."

The problem of evaluating teaching will not go away, and the crosscurrents among the institution, the faculty, and the students keep this matter on the agenda at every school. The dimensions of merit are defined by the local institution, but standardized measures intended to assess teaching competence are likely to blunt instructional diversity and the distinctive characteristics of the individual teacher. Student ratings are a useful source of information for other students and administrators and especially as diagnostic data for the teacher interested in self-improvement. Peer review integrates dimensions of competence that go beyond what students might observe or be qualified to judge—the substance and organization of a course, testing and grading procedures, and intellectual breadth and commitment to teaching, for example. Self-appraisal is continuous, and self-esteem is, in most instances, sufficient to sustain productive effort consistent with one's basic pattern of interacting with students.

Evaluation for purposes of pay and promotion requires conformity to institutionally defined criteria. Each college or university therefore has the responsibility to make available the means for better teaching and to support the efforts of the faculty to meet these local standards and to do so without compromising the special strengths of individual teachers. Problems related to these issues are the focus of Chapter Eleven.

CHAPTER ELEVEN

Institutional Support for Better Teaching

I have been asked to tell the president [of a university], rather presumptuously I fear, what he can do to sustain the quality of my teaching. It never occurred to me that he could do anything. The quality of my teaching is determined by the quality of myself and of my teaching efforts, by my mastery of my subject, by continued study and research, by everlasting diligence in searching for more effective ways of arranging and presenting my knowledge and ideas, and by sensitivity to my effectiveness as a teacher. . . . I do not want more effort devoted to improving teaching; I want more effort devoted to improving learning.   —Professor of physiology

Anyone who wishes to become an artist in education and to know the theory of it must, it will be allowed, betake himself to the universal and get to know it as far as that may be possible.
—Aristotle, *The Ethics*

Despite the combination of budget cuts and soaring costs, schools are finding ways to extend the curriculum, to incorporate new resources for teaching, and to accommodate their educational programs to the changing aims and characteristics of students. The cost of instruction is the big money budget item, but sometimes little money, information, and consultation about technical matters are needed to implement worthwhile change in the way instruction is carried out. College teaching is more complex than it used to be, and each institution has the responsibility of helping its teachers understand what changes might be in order and how to bring them about.

To whom can a teacher turn for current information and support? Teaching is a personal endeavor, and faculty members do not like to go public with their instructional problems—especially those involving feelings of inadequacy. A successful practice in some of the smaller colleges involves designating an individual member of the faculty as a special resource person to whom others can turn for advice and consultation—or simply a sympathetic ear. In making this appointment, the college is showing that it cares about good teaching. This message is stronger if the designated adviser is a respected member of the faculty with earned credibility as an experienced teacher.

Naming a faculty committee on instruction—not a committee for the improvement of instruction—is a larger commitment by the institution, especially if this committee is given a modest budget and clerical assistance. Committee members usually meet the test of credibility because they have experienced firsthand the problems of the classroom; they also participate in faculty governance and engage in research and scholarly writing. Recommendations about teaching from such a group are likely to be better received by the individual teacher than directives from the central administration. Instructional change rarely involves turning square corners because the new element must be incorporated within a teacher's long-standing habits and values. An effective faculty committee knows about and is sensitive to the attitudes and values, the feelings and expectations, that are important to the faculty as a whole.

Admonitions about what teachers "should" and "ought"

to do have less impact than even small amounts of financial support by which, for example, a teacher or a department can purchase reference materials about instruction or initiate a pilot project. In addition, an active faculty committee serves as a coordinating agency for the different units already on campus that do, or might, support instructional development. In a large university, these relevant resources can be extensive: television and audiovisual facilities, computing centers, testing bureaus, and certain departments and individual specialists on topics related to a particular instructional problem.

The Functions of a Center on Teaching

Some type of special support unit for teaching is not uncommon in large universities. Even so, there is no sure formula to ensure that a discriminating faculty will be influenced by the activities of such a unit. This section summarizes lessons learned at the Center for Research on Learning and Teaching at the University of Michigan and from my interchange with counterpart specialists at the other Big Ten midwestern universities. Six main categories of function are briefly reviewed here.

Information About New Developments Related to College Teaching. College professors make their own decisions about how they teach and fine-screen outside sources of information. Preference is given to an analysis of teaching tied closely to their own discipline; the language is familiar and judgments can be made about the credibility of the author. There is no shortage of expertise about teaching, but locally generated statements by administrators, faculty members, or instructional specialists should be written as more than a pedagogical show-and-tell interspersed with educational rhetoric. In addition to specific information, a presentation of the background rationale—the integrating concepts, logic, and data—allows each reader to modify the recipe to meet the situation-specific conditions in a given classroom.

Style of language is a chronic problem. Discipline teachers resist thinking about their own involvement with teaching in the discourse of some other field. Systems engineers have some valuable things to say about teaching and so do psychologists, sociologists, media specialists, psychiatrists, professional educators, philosophers, and poets. We do not need a special educational jargon, but certain general concepts are rich in meaning and help to clarify across the board the nature of the instructional process. The danger is to overuse these borrowed terms—*input, feedback, innovation, instructional systems, role models, creativity, cost benefits,* and the like (present company excepted).

A word about physical appearances is in order. First impressions make a difference, and most of the pieces in the morning mail display the professional touch—written, designed, and printed with the crisp force of a television commercial. The message may not be important, but it is well packaged. Reports to the faculty about research or administrative matters are also well presented. In contrast, information sent out about teaching is often mimeographed or dittoed in overruns beyond the limits of stencil sensitivity. If nothing else, these physical features seem to say that pedagogy is a shoestring operation. And to this I object. Teaching is the central mission of the institution, and information about this function should be presented with the dignity and style it deserves. There is, however, no point in a face-lifting operation if the message is sloppy, fuzzy, or picayune.

Making Special Funds Available for Instructional Development. Advice about teaching is helpful, but money is better; access to funds gives the teacher a little financial elbowroom to try new ways of instruction. A good example of what teachers in large universities like to do by way of instructional change is reported in an annual compendium from the Big Ten universities (Ericksen, 1977). Over 400 instruction-related projects during a fifteen-year period were summarized. About one third involved the use of technological aids, and a comparable proportion were about "instructional rearrangements" for giving greater attention to the individual student. It is clear from these reports that teachers are willing and able to bring about significant improvements when they have access to special funds, information, and consultation.

I suspect that most schools are still looking for the answer to the question of how to give money away to improve instruction. A local educational (or faculty) development fund is often the means for initiating new programs or offering faculty support for study and research during the summer months. One program favored the purchase of hardware, and within two years, the storerooms of participating departments were stacked with all manner of media devices that, after the novelty wore off, gathered dust.

Insofar as the institution's money is specifically geared to instruction, three basic criteria might be brought to bear:

1. Favor proposals that incorporate instructional arrangements not already established in other courses.
2. Design the project so that it can be reviewed while in progress and evaluated by some relevant means at the end.
3. Confirm the home department's intention to use the proposed arrangement if it is judged successful.

On the negative side, funding should be well guarded with respect to purchasing equipment, travel, and faculty salaries because these items can deplete a fund in a hurry. Any set of constraints in the access to money will, of course, be the target of considerable debate.

Workshops and Consultation. This scene prevails at some schools: In a retreat atmosphere, a charismatic person is invited to exhort the faculty about the importance of teaching. Since controversial issues are carefully disguised by euphemisms or set aside, the faculty can sustain congenial spirits. The institutional conscience about teaching is cleared, and the fine fellowship of the faculty will, presumably, carry on. These arrangements fall short of what is needed by way of continuing support for teachers.

Faculty members do not usually talk about their instructional frustrations, conflicts, and feelings of inadequacy—or even their successes. Consequently, teachers sometimes develop a certain feeling of isolation. Given the right arrangement, they appreciate the opportunity to discuss what they actually do as teachers and to pursue, in depth and breadth, various problems pertaining to their careers and responsibilities as members of the faculty. Seminar and workshop sessions provide the means for individual teachers to adapt a new resource for their own courses, to gain practical experience in new modes of teaching, or simply to talk things over with colleagues who share similar interests, values, and problems. In graduate institutions, a carefully considered workshop arrangement is important for guiding the separate departments about the orientation, training, and supervision of the beginning teacher—usually, the graduate student teaching assistant.

A good workshop will usually generate an interest by a few individuals for follow-up consultation or special funds to initiate an instructional experiment. In my view, the highwater mark of a support agency is reached when a staff member sits at the table with a teacher to analyze, for example, the goals for learning in a course, consider how best to use supplementary resources, discuss problems of student motivation, or review testing and grading procedures. Abstractions are set aside while attention is given to how a particular group of students learns and remembers and how their teacher helps.

Upgrading Instructional Technologies. For the foreseeable future, computing will be the dominant technology on campus, but, for the present, its use as an aid for learning will likely call for technical assistance (see Chapter Three). For most courses, software is the immediate frontier as teachers learn how to write programs appropriate for the interaction of students with computer-based presentations. As is true with textbooks, films, and external examinations, commercially available computer software components never quite provide the coverage wanted by the individual teacher. Participation by the teacher is also required to help students over the rough spots troubling them when trying to comprehend new material. Institutional support by way of technical assistance for working out these new instructional skills is well worth the money because the educational benefits of instructional computing will be tremendous.

Certain other aspects of instruction often require special institutional support: test construction, adapting new modes of teaching such as the Personalized System of Instruction (PSI), Audiotutorial, Guided Design, simulation and gaming, Socratic questioning, case-study methods, discussion group techniques, and remedial instruction. Sooner or later, nearly every teacher will benefit from consulting someone knowledgeable about the technical features of particular ways of teaching. In fact, Faris (1979, p. 6) recommends that institutions "provide training programs to ensure that faculty will understand and appreciate the capabilities and limitations of these technologies."

Understanding Student Development. As they have for hundreds of years, teachers influence the character development of students. Today, we are more specific and speak of changes in student attitudes, interests, values, and aspirations. In the process of integrating intellectual development with their social environment, students learn a great deal from each other, and their attitudes and beliefs are significantly shaped and reordered by their teachers. Brown (1965, p. 6) noted, for example, that first-year students "become aware, often for the first time, of the corruption, hypocrisy, and cynicism to be found in a complex society such as ours. It is a challenge to colleges to guide the student through this crisis; to gain the ability to evaluate and judge what is perceived in a way that permits the change but does not lead to complete alienation from previously held truths."

Teachers influence the formation and change of student attitudes and values. The significance of these social factors has been well demonstrated in the development of living and learning arrangements in residence halls as well as in professional training programs (Brown, 1976). "Student development" is an abstract concept but one with concrete and practical manifestations. The contribution of a center on teaching is limited if it cannot bring to the faculty the benefits from the extensive body of research literature and practical experience relating to the personal and social conditions that play such an important role in the academic lives of college students.

The Design of Evaluation Procedures. Fair-and-square evaluation is a ubiquitous and demanding challenge to administrators and teachers (Nevo, 1983). Support in the technical aspects of evaluation procedures is, in some respects, the most critical single contribution from an instructional service unit. The criteria for validating such matters as measures of student achievement, the competence of a teacher, and the quality of an experimental curricular program are often obscure, and consensus judgments about reference standards are hard to come by. The effort to cut through these barriers is essential.

A common pitfall in making an evaluative analysis is to assign too much weight to easily measured elements and to bypass qualitative distinctions: answering factual questions by students receives more attention than demonstrating problem-solving skills, short-term appeals in teaching have precedence over the long-term impact, and a cost-effective curricular program is given priority over one that strengthens the value systems of students. Similar contrasts can be drawn from many other aspects of evaluative efforts such as effects of special instruction in the basic skills, assessing faculty attitudes, and determining the transfer of learning effects from particular courses.

The procedures used in making evaluative judgment should be explicitly stated in the final report, in the interest of educational justice by way of interpretation. The design for deriving the evaluation of an instructional experiment, for example, should be part of the initial proposal. Too many compromises must be made if "evaluation" is tacked on at the end of a project report. A third party, such as a staff member at the instructional support unit, is a valuable resource for working out these complicated evaluation procedures.

Maintaining Credibility

Good service from an instructional support unit reflects good research: the ability to untangle and assess the essential factors in an instructional problem and to bring relevant data, concepts, and procedural considerations to bear. Since subject-matter teachers do this within their own field of specialization, they look for and appreciate corresponding competence from their consultants. College faculty members will have reservations about seeking help if they are only encouraged, in effect, to tinker with teaching, manipulate technological "innovations," and perform stage tricks on the podium and testing tricks on students. If a teacher is concerned about the motivation of students, for example, then the consultant should know more about the theory, concepts, and research relating to student dynamics than the biology (or chemistry or philosophy) teacher asking the question. The same is true about other matters: assessing student performance, teaching abstract concepts, exploring how attitudes and values are formed (and changed), and using technological teaching aids to the best advantage. If a support unit does not do its homework of research, its credibility will soon be thoroughly erased.

From research-based information and the reported experiences of others, a support unit can go beyond the reactive role of responding to the requests from teachers, committees, and administrators and take an advocating position, pressing for better ways of teaching. The suggested instructional arrangement may not sell at first, but the faculty will at least respect the challenge from a well-founded source. Demonstrated leadership in research and development related to college-level instruction will inevitably strengthen the quality of a service program and sustain its credibility.

To recapitulate, when a teacher finally reaches the point when he or she is willing to raise a hand asking for help, the support unit should be there to do something about it—either directly or via its coordinating function for other resources on campus or elsewhere. A center on teaching should be viewed by the faculty as the one door for finding assistance to resolve a here-and-now problem in the teacher's own classroom. In effect, such a center serves as an instructional research laboratory (or clinic) from which findings can be reported for the benefit of other teachers to other departments, if not to other schools.

The location of the center in an institution's organizational chart is less important than the strength of its supporting resources. The credibility of the staff is enhanced when these men and women hold joint appointments in a teaching department and thus work in the same academic forum as their faculty colleagues—to teach, serve on faculty committees, attend and participate in faculty meetings, and publish or perish along with their associates. Even so, a policy committee of respected members of the faculty will remind staff specialists of the sensitivities and opinions about teaching that are important to the faculty as a whole. A policy committee also serves as an effective link to the governance structure in the school that is so often involved with important considerations about teaching.

Cooperation About Teaching Among Institutions

Colleges and universities know well how to compete with one another, but they are finding that cooperation has its advantages. Institutional autonomy is one thing but provincialism is something else, and every school can benefit from lessons learned about instruction elsewhere. The Committee on Institutional Cooperation—with representatives from the Big Ten universities and the University of Chicago—is a good example of a regional interchange. These universities have been working together since 1959.

One of the committee's task groups, the Panel for Research and Development of Instructional Resources, was started in 1964; for sixteen years, it published an annual compendium, *Development and Experiment in College Teaching* (Ericksen, 1966-1981), for distribution to administrators and faculty at the participating schools. A review of this sequence of reports shows the changing nature of interinstitutional cooperation on matters pertaining to instruction. At first, the pages were filled with accounts of particular classroom projects initiated by subject-matter teachers. Gradually the emphasis changed to descriptions of larger and more comprehensive programs under way at the member schools: improving the basic skills of reading and writing required of college students, curricular changes for subgroups of students, and interinstitutional use of media resources and computing technology.

Sustained interaction by essentially the same group of participants is probably essential for working out the similarities and the differences between particular school-based programs, the articulation between high school and college, remediation arrangements, meeting the needs of adult learners, adapting computer technology for local instruction, and experiential education, for example. A one-shot conference is adequate only for marking the boundaries of a general instructional problem. Repeated discussions, on the other hand, allow the participants to penetrate the generalized statements and to examine the mechanisms likely to lead to constructive action.

The cost of instruction is the major budget item at most schools, and it makes good sense to protect this investment. One means is to provide concrete support for individual teachers wanting to do a better job. Variations of a center on teaching can contribute by providing information about new developments related to college teaching, managing special funds for teacher-initiated instructional projects, offering workshops and consultation, guiding the best use of the media technologies and computer-based instruction, and working with individual teachers, departments, and larger units on problems related to student development—attitude and value change, motivation, aspirations, and the like. A critically significant contribution is consultation regarding the making of evaluative judgments about students, teachers, and programs.

The credibility of these service functions is enhanced when based on active programs of research related to instructional problems. Interinstitutional cooperation is a cost-effective way of reducing the provincialism of teaching and is most effective when based on the sustained interaction by a given group of participants. Sustaining the enthusiasm and competence of the individual teacher is another, and final, matter.

CHAPTER TWELVE

Sustaining Good Teaching over Time

And if a teacher is to maintain a healthy self-esteem throughout his career, I see no substitute for the proof of worth that comes with original, creative research. The alternative may be a faculty member who loses his nerve in mid-career and shrinks from the classroom as if from a pit of dragons. Or it may be someone who turns to such shabby ploys as assuming the mantle of standup comic or student confidant. The latter approaches may even win temporary applause; in later years the students will realize they have been defrauded.

—Professor of law

The work of being a teacher is sustained from many sources, but three pervade the academic lives of most teachers most of the time: We treasure our autonomy and guard our individuality, enjoy the interactive company of students and peers, and feel satisfied when knowing we are contributing to goals of the institution. These motivating states are part of the inside story threading through career diaries from our apprenticeship days, through midcareer, and during the countdown years to retirement. Csikszentmihalyi (1982) makes a strong statement about the overriding significance of motivation. "Higher education succeeds or fails in terms of motivation, not cognitive transfer of information. . . . The best way to get students to believe that it makes sense to pursue knowledge is to believe in it oneself. Thus, an effective professor is one who is intrinsically motivated to learn, because it is he or she who will have the best chance to educate others" (pp. 15-16).

The basic dynamics of students are in parallel because they also treasure personal freedom, the society of other students, and satisfaction in moving toward their educational goals. The motivational commonality is matched by the fact that students and teachers think alike; the mental processes by which teachers manage information are the same as those at work when students learn, understand, and remember. Maehr and Kleiber (1981) confirm the continuity of achievement motivation from youthful students to older teachers. This similarity in motivation and thinking is intrinsic to the interchange called "teaching" and is the prime resource for sustaining zest and enthusiasm for teaching over the long haul.

The substance of instruction bridges the wisdom of the past with the future purposes of students: F_1 talking with F_2 generation about information, procedures, and points of view that are judged to stand the test of time. My analysis of the measure of good teaching has largely been anchored to the instructional connections between motivation and learning. Understanding this fundamental relationship is more relevant than is information about the techniques of instruction. Teachers who continue to enjoy their work are more likely to be those who stay in tune with the former and worry only a little about the latter.

The greenhouse college environment is not without doors, windows, and outside sources of nutriments. The campus community is sensitive to what is going on outside, and teachers change *what* they teach in keeping abreast of new developments. They change *how* they teach as experience strengthens their understanding of the primary factors influencing how students learn and remember and how attitudes and values are formed.

Apprentice Teachers

Beginning teachers are not yet being distracted by complications that impinge on older teachers: intra- and interdepartmental power plays, competition in research and publications, conflicts about faculty governance, curricular hassles, and the not too subtle display of academic status symbols. It is revealing, therefore, to look at beginning teachers as a relatively clear instance of the sustaining dimension of teaching.

Most of us moved to the other side of the desk as graduate student teaching assistants. For several years, I enjoyed a supervisor's ringside seat for observing the frustrations and the satisfactions of apprentice teachers. For six years, the Center for Research on Learning and Teaching (CRLT) sponsored a program for the orientation and supervision of teaching assistants (TAs) in five large departments—philosophy, botany, physics, psychology, and history—and follow-up work with most of the other major graduate departments. These experiences confirmed the two major findings of an earlier survey (Koen and Ericksen, 1967) of the role of TAs in fifty large universities: (1) successful TA training programs received active support from the power structure within the department and (2) advanced and experienced TAs were especially effective as supervisors in the in-service training of beginning TAs.

Good teachers are more born than made—at least, by a crash training program. Full advantage should be taken of the self-selection process by those who have reason to believe that they would find satisfaction as teachers. Most have a solid basis for this opinion because, as students, they have been spectators to the teaching process for many years and have witnessed, first-hand, various styles and personalities. They have seen what it takes to derive satisfaction in this kind of work. Nevertheless, anxiety is the keynote affective state for beginning teachers—"Will I be liked by my students and earn their confidence and respect?" A phase-in program by the department or school is nearly always in order.

A balanced formal program for the orientation and training of starting teachers has two main components: a preliminary briefing and in-service training. Preservice sessions are mainly geared to providing information about the instructional policies of the institution and the department. This translates into explanations about pay, security, autonomy, testing and grading, and access to supplementary resources. Apprentice teachers also want to be informed about matters relating to roles, status, responsibilities, rights, and privileges. The functional meaning of these policies becomes clear during the on-the-job experiences in the in-service training and supervision. Formally recognized or not, experience is the best teacher about teaching. The early weeks of actual teaching are a time when the beginner senses the points of congruence and dissonance between one's own habits and personal qualities and those of students. In-service training encourages discussions about the specific skills of teaching and the opportunity for the supervisor to forestall misunderstanding, frustration, and bitterness when day-by-day experiences are at variance with expectations.

In personal conversations and in group discussions, most beginning teachers talk openly about their feelings and freely exchange information about their classroom experiences. A supervisor can note the growing identification of TAs with the teaching role, expressions of rapport with students, and signs of satisfaction with their accomplishments. Often a TA's progress toward the Ph.D. degree is slowed as involvement with the affairs of teaching takes precedence over dissertation research. The specifics vary from one person to the next, but beginning teachers find support and encouragement from, basically, the same conditions that will sustain their efforts through the later teaching career: preserving individual autonomy, the interchange with others, and feeling a sense of competence in managing a course of study.

Dimensions of Merit in Midcareer

Teachers on a tenure-track appointment are concerned about knowing what kind of performance is expected for earning salary increases and promotion. One crass view is to consider the institution as a pellet machine molding and shaping the behavior of its hired hands. It would, of course, be both shortsighted and foolish to minimize the importance of institutional recognition and reward, but these mechanisms are lessened in value when they become predictable or seem only slightly related to what teachers actually do. Extrinsic rewards misjudge or overlook powerful factors in the career life of the self-sustaining professor. In their perceptive analysis of the progress of academic careers, Baldwin and Blackburn (1981) indicate various modes of institutional support for teachers at different stages of professional development.

Self-esteem is the dimension of merit that counts the most over the career years. Of course, self-esteem is nourished by institutional recognition and support, but even the practice of making awards for superior teaching has limited value. Winning a special award for "outstanding" teaching feels good to the recipients (they tell me), but the very general descriptive language gives little guidance to the journeyman teacher. To set one's sights on winning a teaching award may not lead to the same instructional action as striving to have a long-term impact on what students carry away from a course of study. Winning a prize as an outstanding teacher brings prestige to the individual but, for the rest of us, it mainly suggests that the institution cares about "good teaching"—relatively undefined. Let it rest at that.

With two of my associates at CRLT (Ericksen, Moore, and Lawrence, 1978), in-depth interviews were held with sixty-five teachers in the College of Literature, Science, and the Arts. In effect, we asked what they did, or are now doing, to advance their careers in the university. Using interviews, rather than a questionnaire, enabled us to pursue more accurately the factors that individual teachers perceive as critical; we could ask follow-up questions and clarify our interpretation of some of the involved responses. (Questionnaires have limited value for probing complex matters involving the interplay of feelings and values.) The interviews, conducted in the summer and fall of 1976, included all those appointed as assistant professors in the years 1960, 1965, and 1970; this span of years covered periods of institutional expansion as well as a time of leveling off.

The interviews were scheduled for ninety minutes, but most went on for a longer time—some for three or four hours. We made no attempt to gather data from those who had left the university because our purpose was to find out about the motivational profile for those teachers who were then carrying out the educational affairs of the university. Many of the professors with whom we talked have been, are, or probably will be members of a department executive committee and, in this role, their opinions have the force of policy.

Main Findings from Interviews. On the average, this group estimated that, as assistant professors, close to half their time was given to teaching. The variations in this distribution of effort were considerable, ranging from 20 to 80 percent for teaching and from 5 to 75 percent for research. The main change following promotion to associate professor and then on to full professor was a slight increase in time given to service activities.

We asked, "What is the relative weight given to research, teaching, and service for promotion in your department?" Research was clearly dominant—both in their perceptions about actual weight and their preferences about how these functions should be weighed. The preference judgments, however, showed a slight shift toward a closer balance among research, teaching, and service. The results were essentially the same when asked about promotion to full professor.

When the query was made, "What has been the basis for your own advancement?," the most striking difference was the comparison among the groups of faculty appointed at different times. The 1960 group judged that their research was a factor of about 42 percent in their promotion to associate professor, but this value was stepped up to 68 percent for the 1970 group. A similar shift was shown in the promotion to full professor.

Most of those in our sample (88 percent) believed that significant changes had taken place since the time of their initial appointment. In their view, the criteria are now more stringent and department expectations regarding research and scholarly productivity have risen.

It is both easy and acceptable to blame involvement in research for poor teaching. Only on occasion, however, was this conflict presented in our interviews. The great majority indicated that they found their participation in research and teaching to be basically complementary. Many of the findings and ideas they emphasized in teaching were a direct outgrowth of their research and, as a result, instruction was infused with fresh perspectives and new material. The overall picture was one of *a close and constructive interrelationship between teaching and research.* Of particular interest was the finding that almost half of those with whom we talked reported that their research and teaching became more mutually supportive over time. In the first few years, they were teaching broad, introductory-level courses and pursuing narrow, highly specific research with little classroom overlap. With the passage of time, however, their teaching activities shifted to advanced courses, and their research or scholarly pursuits often broadened beyond the bounds of earlier interests and became more relevant to what they were teaching.

There appears to be a fairly consistent relationship between the extent to which a faculty member is able to intermesh research and teaching activities and the extent to which he or she is rewarded by the department with promotion and increases in salary. Those in our sample whom we identified as being among the most well rewarded by the institution almost without exception reported that they found their teaching and research activities complementary. On the other hand, those who had found these activities basically competitive were among the least rewarded by the institution. Apparently, those faculty members who have achieved the most satisfactory situation at the university are those who have been able to integrate their teaching and research activities.

The amount of satisfaction that faculty members derived from each of their career activities seems to reflect the amount of time devoted to a given activity. One exception was the frequent observation that "I spend about half my energies on teaching but receive considerably more than half my satisfaction from my work with students." At the assistant professor level, teaching provided somewhat more satisfaction (47 percent) than research (38 percent), while service (12 percent) was well down the line. At the higher ranks, teachers spent more time in service affairs and reported some increase in the satisfaction derived from such activities. In general, teaching tended to be viewed as giving short-term satisfaction, whereas the positive feelings derived from research and scholarship were considered more enduring.

Implications for the Self-Sustaining Professor. The interviewed teachers reported a shift over time in the balance of external and internal pressures that they experienced. Prior to achieving tenure, the faculty often felt considerable pressure to be visibly productive in ways that have immediate payoffs— products that were often defined by the needs and interests of the department. Following tenure, faculty members experienced fewer constraints and felt they were able to pursue their own interests in greater depth. This freedom to develop a particular line of inquiry must surely be one of the major educational strengths of a good university.

Each member of the faculty has strong opinions about what the dimensions of merit are and what they should be. Most have adapted successfully to the system and seem to accept its values when they talk about why they do research, how it affects their teaching, and how these and other self-directed activities combine into a self-sustaining career.

In essence, these interviews indicate that career satisfaction derives in good measure from the freedom teachers experience to control what and how they teach and to pursue self-initiated areas of intellectual inquiry. The university is not perceived as a monolithic institution at all, but one that encourages and recognizes a great diversity of faculty activities and achievements. Although changes are taking place in the merit criteria for promotion, the principle of competence remains steadfast. In one way or another, our interview sample indicated that pay increases and promotion are not, in themselves, sufficient incentives to maintain consistently good instruction. The personal standards of the teacher do more to sustain week-by-week, year-by-year effective performance in the classroom. Pay, promotion, and tenure are housekeeping arrangements—necessary but not sufficient. If you do not believe me, talk with a person who has been teaching a long time.

From Age Sixty Onward

The faculty of the future will be older, and if older teachers want company, they will have it. It is to the institution's advantage to consider how best to make use of the special competence of senior professors for meeting current problems of teaching, research, and service. The detractors to this contribution are many and persistent but one hurdle stands high: the stereotype of older teachers as tired and conservative. The literature reflects this negative view, and most of the reports examine ways institutions can increase flexibility for moving younger people in and older people around and out, to counter "tired old blood" with "vigorous new blood."

From age sixty to seventy are capstone years, and these senior professors see the university "steadily and see it whole." They know the academic score and offer many confirming examples of what it takes to sustain oneself as a teacher. They are quite aware of what they do well and the nature of their limitation; certainly, they do not want to be pampered and are, in fact, wary of administrative action that might be seen as having a paternalistic or manipulative tone. Skinner's (1983) appraisal of his own process of aging includes some admonishments appropriate for older teachers, "Beware of those who are trying to be helpful and too readily flatter you . . . those who help those who can help themselves work a sinister kind of destruction by making the good things in life no longer properly contingent on behavior" (p. 244).

Older teachers resist innuendos about "deadwood" because they know full well that incompetence is not an age-linked condition. Deadwood is seen among TAs, all ranks of teachers, and the administration. Age is an irrelevant criterion for judging the contribution of a teacher; on the other hand, it is the natural line to follow for finding factors that sustain a teacher through the years.

One of the more encouraging results from research on

aging is the persistence of intellectual vigor. After fifty, slippage occurs on the periphery of the body—eyeglasses, hearing aids, dentures, canes, and knowing where the restrooms are—but the central mental power remains on par with the more athletic juniors. Older teachers know their subjects in depth and in breadth; they understand students and have a discriminating perspective about the relations between academia and the larger social world. It is particularly insidious, therefore, when older teachers accept the prevailing but pejorative stereotypes that they are becoming inept or in the way.

The best institutional countermove is to make opportunities available whereby these older men and women can demonstrate the educational wisdom that comes with age. Certain specific and concrete steps take advantage of the self-sustaining strengths of older teachers for serving the educational interests of the college or university:

1. Extending teaching into new sites—visiting and exchange professorships are more readily worked out with teachers less encumbered with children in school. To step outside the home department is, to an experienced teacher, a challenge rather than a threat.

2. Offering new interdisciplinary courses—in the security and confidence of their status, senior professors can take the lead in updating the curriculum in this manner.

3. Mentorships in research, teaching, and service—many older teachers have invaluable experience that can be turned to the benefit of younger staff members.

4. Initiating experimental instructional projects—older teachers are less constrained by conventional modes for managing the classroom hour than are promotion-conscious assistant professors; they are more willing to realize, finally, long-suppressed instructional desires.

5. A faculty forum for those who have been teaching many years—this could be a useful sounding board for institutional policies and practices for sustaining productive careers on the part of the larger faculty.

Each of these illustrative ventures builds on the special talents of older teachers and takes advantage of their strong identification with the home school and their desire to end their careers on a high note.

Self-Esteem

Teachers work in a dual-track system: extrinsic recognition and reward from the institution and the intrinsic satisfaction directly given by the experience of teaching (Bess, 1982). The boundary between the two meanders and is permeable. One teacher may be autonomous and self-sufficient with respect to research but lean on institutional mechanisms for sustenance and support as a teacher. Others reverse the dependency but both sets of factors give balance to self-esteem.

Immediate versus delayed recognition is another contrast related to sustaining self-esteem. The outside rewards for research and writing come later—if at all—but teaching is a means for daily reinforcement. The institutional criteria for excellence are not well defined and are, certainly, not uniform across departments. Older teachers have learned how to ride these out and are not confused about priorities as they go about successfully managing the classroom hour. Earning tenure or receiving a salary boost does not make much difference in the specifics of a teacher's classroom performance but positive signals from students do. Some of the younger and less secure teachers succumb to the temptation of receiving daily strokes and reach out for these by making dramatic statements, cute comments, and humorous quips or by engaging in intellectual posturing. These teachers usually burn out with the passage of time.

It is rewarding to see the impressive display of knowledge shown by students on a comprehensive final examination, but greater satisfaction derives from confidence that the answers to some of these questions will endure. A mature teacher is reassured in knowing that he or she has initiated a significant learning chain reaction, that private knowledge will continue to expand as students live and learn away from the classroom.

Over the years, the work of teaching may sap your energy but not your enthusiasm; your office may become worn and dingy but not the message that you hold forth; your colleagues may have lost some of their stimulus value but not so with your students. If you have seen one student, you have seen only one, and you engage with hundreds of such individuals over the course of a teaching career. There is something intrinsically vitalizing about the minds and motives of individual students preparing for the years ahead. Several times each year we face a new group of individuals interested in traveling a route they have not been on before, which we update and extend each time around. The questions change and the answers change; no course is dull if we keep our subject alive by making it relevant to the future. Success in this interchange will enhance self-esteem and therefore sustain the good teacher.

The Final Word

Come the revolution, teachers will be the first to be taken from the scene since they have such a powerful influence on the next generation. In the meantime, enjoy your prophetic work as, by precept and example, you reshape accumulated knowledge to help students achieve the aims of their own education. College instruction is becoming more complicated as new objectives and new resources enter the scene. In any case, curiosity leading to understanding is the key motive managed by teachers because curiosity keeps students at it—rehearsing what they learn as the means for fitting new information into their permanent store of knowledge. To this end, the concepts students comprehend are more vital than the styles of teaching they observe. Learning how to think independently is the most important end product of education and is helped along by the teacher as counselor, mentor, and friend. The fair and equitable assessment of student achievement is a necessary condition for educational justice, and the return of diagnostic information is especially helpful as an aid for learning. Teachers likewise deserve valid evaluations—including diagnostic information about their own strengths and limitations. Teachers appreciate ready access to institutional support for helping them do a better job; knowing one is improving as a teacher sustains one's efforts over the career years.

Compared to the rest of the world, the college campus is a delightful place to work, and most teachers would not trade places with any other profession. They know they may never be a hero, but for some students they will have made a difference and this contribution is hard to beat.

References

Abrami, P. C., Leventhal, L., and Perry, R. P. "Educational Seduction." *Review of Educational Research*, 1982, *52*(3), 446-464.

Baldwin, R. G., and Blackburn, R. T. "The Academic Career As a Developmental Process." *Journal of Higher Education*, 1981, *52*(6).

Bartlett, F. C. *Remembering: A Study in Experimental and Social Psychology.* Cambridge, England: Cambridge University Press, 1932.

Bellezza, F. S. "Mnemonic Devices: Classification, Characteristics, and Criteria." *Review of Educational Research*, 1981, *51*(2), 247-275.

Bellezza, F. S. "Updating Memory Using Mnemonic Devices." *Cognitive Psychology*, 1982, *14*, 301-327.

Bergman, C. A., Rubenstein, S. L., and Dunn, R. F. "Writing in the 1980s: Three Views." *Bulletin of the American Association for Higher Education*, 1982, *35*(4), 3-8.

167

Bess, J. L. (Ed.). *New Directions for Teaching and Learning: Motivating Professors to Teach Effectively,* no. 10. San Francisco: Jossey-Bass, 1982.

Bjork, R. A. "Information-Processing Analysis of College Teaching." *Educational Psychologist,* 1979, *14,* 15–23.

Bloom, B. S. Untitled statement in F. H. Farley (Ed.), "The Future of Educational Research." *Educational Researcher,* 1982, *11*(8), 12–13.

Bordin, E. S. "The Teacher As a Counselor." *Memo to the Faculty,* No. 38. Ann Arbor: Center for Research on Learning and Teaching, University of Michigan, 1969.

Bransford, J. D. *Human Cognition: Learning, Understanding, and Remembering.* Belmont, Calif.: Wadsworth, 1979.

Brown, D. R. "Personality, Environment, and Academic Achievement." *Memo to the Faculty,* No. 9. Ann Arbor: Center for Research on Learning and Teaching, University of Michigan, 1965.

Brown, D. R. "A Longitudinal Program of Evaluation of Socialization and Achievement in Medical, Legal, and Liberal Arts Programs." In D. Graijter, J. Vander Kamp, and H. Crombag (Eds.), *Prospects in Psychological and Educational Measurement.* New York: Wiley, 1976.

Centra, J. A. *Determining Faculty Effectiveness: Assessing Teaching, Research, and Service for Personnel Decisions and Improvement.* San Francisco: Jossey-Bass, 1979.

Champagne, A. B., Klopfer, L. E., and Gunstone, R. F. "Cognitive Research and the Design of Science Instruction." *Educational Psychologist,* 1982, *17*(1), 31–53.

Chickering, A. W. "Grades: One More Tilt at the Windmill." *Bulletin of the American Association for Higher Education,* 1983, *35*(8), 10–13.

Chomsky, N. *Language and Mind.* New York: Harcourt Brace Jovanovich, 1972.

Cohen, P. A. "Effectiveness of Student-Rating Feedback for Improving College Instruction: A Meta-Analysis of Findings." *Research in Higher Education,* Vol. 4. New York: Agathon Press, 1980.

Cohen, P. A. "Validity of Student Ratings in Psychology Courses:

A Research Synthesis." *Teaching of Psychology,* 1982, *9*(2), 78-82.

Cohen, P. A., and McKeachie, W. J. "The Role of Colleagues in the Evaluation of College Teaching." *Improving College and University Teaching,* 1980, *8*(4), 147-154.

Cronbach, L. J., and Snow, R. E. *Aptitudes and Instructional Methods: A Handbook for Research on Interactions.* New York: Irvington, 1977.

Cross, K. P. "Not *Can* but *Will* College Teaching Be Improved?" In J. A. Centra (Ed.), *New Directions for Higher Education: Renewing and Evaluating Teaching,* no. 17. San Francisco: Jossey-Bass, 1977.

Cross, K. P. (Ed.). *Underprepared Learners: Current Issues in Higher Education.* Washington, D.C.: American Association for Higher Education, 1982-1983.

Csikszentmihalyi, M. "Intrinsic Motivation and Effective Teaching: A Flow Analysis." In J. L. Bess (Ed.), *New Directions for Teaching and Learning: Motivating Professors to Teach Effectively,* no. 10. San Francisco: Jossey-Bass, 1982.

Dessler, A. J. (Ed.). *Proceedings of Keller Method Workshop Conference.* Houston: Rice University, 1972.

diSibio, M. "Memory for Connected Discourse: A Constructivist View." *Review of Educational Research,* 1982, *52*(2), 149-174.

Eble, K. E. "Teaching Styles and Faculty Behaviors." In K. E. Eble (Ed.), *New Directions for Teaching and Learning: Improving Teaching Styles,* no. 1. San Francisco: Jossey-Bass, 1980.

Ericksen, S. C. "Studies in the Abstraction Process." *Psychological Monographs,* 1962, *76*(18, whole no. 537).

Ericksen, S. C. *Motivation for Learning: A Guide for the Teacher of the Young Adult.* Ann Arbor: University of Michigan Press, 1974.

Ericksen, S. C. "Restless Teachers and Institutional Support for Change." *Educational Psychologist,* 1977, *12*(2), 207-214.

Ericksen, S. C. (Ed.). *Development and Experiment in College Teaching.* An annual compendium (Reports 1-16) prepared by the Committee on Instructional Cooperation, Panel on

Research and Development of Instructional Resources. Ann Arbor: Center for Research on Learning and Teaching, University of Michigan, 1966-1981.

Ericksen, S. C., Moore, W. E., and Lawrence, J. H. "The Dimensions of Merit." *Memo to the Faculty,* No. 61. Ann Arbor: Center for Research on Learning and Teaching, University of Michigan, 1978.

Ericsson, K. A., and Chase, W. G. "Exceptional Memory." *American Scientist,* 1982, *70*(6), 607-615.

Faris, G. K. "Instructional Technology." In S. C. Ericksen and J. A. Cook (Eds.), *Support for Teaching at Major Universities.* Ann Arbor: Center for Research on Learning and Teaching, University of Michigan, 1979.

Frase, L. T. (Ed.). "Special Issue: The Psychology of Writing." *Educational Psychologist,* 1982, *17*(whole no. 3).

Frederiksen, N. "The Real Test Bias: Influences of Testing on Teaching and Learning." *American Psychologist,* 1984, *39* (3), 193-202.

Fuhrman, B. S., and Grasha, A. F. *A Practical Handbook for College Teachers.* Boston: Little, Brown, 1983.

Gagné, R. M. "Is Educational Technology in Phase?" *Educational Technology,* 1980, *20*(2), 7-14.

Gagné, R. M. "An Interview on Implications for Instructional Design and Development." *Educational Technology,* 1982, *22* (6), 11-15.

Glaser, R. "The Bridge Between the Learning Laboratory and the Classroom: Discussion." *Educational Psychologist,* 1973, *10*(3), 129-132.

Glaser, R. "Instructional Psychology: Past, Present, and Future." *American Psychologist,* 1982, *37*(3), 292-305.

Glaser, R. "Education and Thinking: The Role of Knowledge." *American Psychologist,* 1984, *39*(2), 93-104.

Greeno, J. G. "Theory and Practice Regarding Acquired Cognitive Structures." *Educational Psychologist,* 1973, *10*(3), 117-122.

Greeno, J. G. "Responses to Phillips." *Educational Psychologist,* 1983, *18*(2), 75-80.

Hunt, E. "On the Nature of Intelligence." *Science,* 1983, *219* (4581), 141-146.

Hyman, H. H., Wright, C. R., and Reed, J. S. *The Enduring Ef-fects of Education.* Chicago: University of Chicago Press, 1975.

Jenness, A. "Mark Hopkins and Stanley Hall on a Log: Facts and Fables About the APA Founder's Psychology Teacher." Address to 72nd annual meeting of the American Psychological Association, Los Angeles, 1964.

Judge, C. A. "The Academic Counseling Office of the College of Literature, Science, and the Arts." *Memo to the Faculty,* No. 69. Ann Arbor: Center for Research on Learning and Teaching, University of Michigan, 1981.

Koen, F., and Ericksen, S. C. "Analysis of the Specific Features Which Characterize the More Successful Programs for the Recruitment and Training of College Teachers." *Memo to the Faculty,* No. 21. Ann Arbor: Center for Research on Learning and Teaching, University of Michigan, 1967.

Korn, H. A. "Some Observations on Counseling for College Students." *Memo to the Faculty,* No. 69. Ann Arbor: Center for Research on Learning and Teaching, University of Michigan, 1981.

Kulik, J. A. "Student Reactions to Instruction." *Memo to the Faculty,* No. 58. Ann Arbor: Center for Research on Learning and Teaching, University of Michigan, 1976.

Kulik, J. A. "Individualized Systems of Instruction." In H. E. Mitzel (Ed.), *The Encyclopedia of Educational Research.* New York: Macmillan, 1983.

Kulik, J. A., and McKeachie, W. J. "The Evaluation of Teachers in Higher Education." In F. N. Kerlinger (Ed.), *Review of Research in Education,* Vol. 3. Itasca, Ill.: Peacock, 1975.

Larkin, J. H., Heller, J. I., and Greeno, J. G. "Instructional Implications of Research on Problem Solving." In W. J. McKeachie (Ed.), *New Directions for Teaching and Learning: Learning, Cognition, and College Teaching,* no. 2. San Francisco: Jossey-Bass, 1980.

Lawrence, J. H. *Descriptions of Exemplary Teachers—An Exploratory Study of Awards.* Ann Arbor: Center for Research on Learning and Teaching, University of Michigan, 1982.

Lazarus, R. S. "Thoughts on the Relations Between Emotion

and Cognition." *American Psychologist,* 1982, *37*(9), 1019-1024.

Locke, J. "Some Thoughts Concerning Education." In P. Gay (Ed.), *John Locke on Education.* New York: Bureau of Publications, Teachers College, Columbia University, 1964. (Originally published in London, 1693.)

McKeachie, W. J. "The Decline and Fall of the Laws of Learning." *Educational Researcher,* 1974, *3*(3), 7-11.

Maehr, M. L., and Kleiber, D. A. "The Graying of Achievement Motivation." *American Psychologist,* 1981, *36*(7), 787-793.

Marsh, H. W. "Factors Affecting Students' Evaluations of the Same Course Taught by the Same Instructor on Different Occasions." *American Educational Research Journal,* 1982, *19*(4), 485-497.

Messick, S. "Evidence and Ethics in the Evaluation of Tests." *Educational Researcher,* 1981, *10*(9), 9-20.

Milton, O., and Edgerly, J. W. *The Testing and Grading of Students.* New Rochelle, N.Y.: *Change* Magazine, 1976.

Naftulin, C. H., Ware, J. E., and Connelly, F. A. "The Doctor Fox Lecture: A Paradigm of Educational Seduction." *Journal of Medical Education,* 1973, *48,* 630-635.

Neisser, U. *Cognition and Reality—Principles and Implications of Cognitive Psychology.* New York: W. H. Freeman, 1976.

Nelkin, D. "Intellectual Property: The Control of Scientific Information." *Science,* 1982, *216,* 704-708.

Nevo, D. "The Conceptualization of Educational Evaluation: An Analytical Review of the Literature." *Review of Educational Research,* 1983, *53*(1), 117-128.

Norman, D. A. "What Goes on in the Mind of the Learner?" In W. J. McKeachie (Ed.), *New Directions for Teaching and Learning: Learning, Cognition, and College Teaching,* no. 2. San Francisco: Jossey-Bass, 1980.

Overall, J. J., and Marsh, H. W. "Students' Evaluations of Teaching: An Update." *Bulletin of the American Association for Higher Education,* 1982, *35*(4), 9-12.

Peek, G. S. "Grading by Jury: Accurate and Consistent." *Improving College and University Teaching,* 1982, *30*(2), 75-79.

Persig, R. M. *Zen and the Art of Motorcycle Maintenance: An Inquiry into Values.* New York: Morrow, 1974.

Plato. *Phaedrus.* (W. C. Helmbold and W. G. Rabinowitz, Trans.) New York: Bobbs-Merrill, 1956.

Raben, J. "Advent of the Post-Gutenberg University." *Academe,* 1983, *69*(2), 21-27.

Reif, F., and Heller, J. I. "Knowledge Structure and Problem Solving in Physics." *Educational Psychologist,* 1982, *17*(2), 102-127.

Reiser, R. A., and Gagné, R. M. "Characteristics of Media Selection Models." *Review of Educational Research,* 1983, *52* (4), 499-512.

Resnick, L. B. "Mathematics and Science Learning: A New Conception." *Science,* 1983, *221,* 477-478.

Rosenbaum, R. A., and others. "Academic Freedom and the Classified Information System." *Science,* 1983, *219*(4582), 257-259.

Rothkopf, E. Z. "Course Content and Supportive Environments for Learning." *Educational Psychologist,* 1973, *10*(3), 123-128.

Rowntree, D. *Assessing Students: How Shall We Know Them?* New York: Harper & Row, 1977.

Sampson, G. W., and others. "Academic and Occupational Performance: A Quantitative Synthesis." *American Educational Research Journal,* 1984, *21*(2), 311-321.

Schrader, W. B. (Ed.). *New Directions for Testing and Measurement: Measuring Achievement: Progress over a Decade,* no. 5. (Proceedings of the 1979 Educational Testing Service Invitational Conference.) San Francisco: Jossey-Bass, 1980.

Seibert, W. F. "Student Evaluations of Instruction." In S. C. Ericksen and J. A. Cook (Eds.), *Support for Teaching at Major Universities.* Ann Arbor: Center for Research on Learning and Teaching, University of Michigan, 1979.

Sheffield, E. F. *Teaching in the Universities: No One Way.* Montreal: McGill-Queen's Press, 1974.

Sherman, A. R. "Psychology Fieldwork: A Catalyst for Advancing Knowledge and Academic Skills." *Teaching of Psychology,* 1982, *9*(2), 82-85.

Skinner, B. F. "The Science of Learning and the Art of Teaching." *Harvard Educational Review,* 1954, *24,* 86-97.

Skinner, B. F. "Intellectual Self-Management in Old Age." *American Psychologist,* 1983, *38*(3), 239-244.

Snow, R. E., and Peterson, P. L. "Recognizing Differences in Student Aptitude." In W. J. McKeachie (Ed.), *New Directions for Teaching and Learning: Learning, Cognition, and College Teaching,* no. 2. San Francisco: Jossey-Bass, 1980.

Stanners, R. F., and Brown, L. T. "Conceptual Relationships Based on Learning in Introductory Psychology." *Teaching of Psychology,* 1982, *9*(2), 74-77.

Stoan, S. K. "Computer Searching: A Primer for the Uninformed Scholar." *Academe,* 1982, *68*(6), 10-20.

Strange, J. H. "Preparing for Today Tomorrow: Faculty Training for the New Technologies." *Bulletin of the American Association for Higher Education,* 1983, *36*(2), 10-14.

Thune, L. E., and Ericksen, S. C. *Studies in Abstraction Learning: IV. The Transfer Effects of Conceptual Versus Rote Instruction in a Simulated Classroom Situation.* Office of Naval Research Technical Report No. 6. Nashville, Tenn.: Vanderbilt University, 1960.

Tobias, S. "When Do Instructional Methods Make a Difference?" *Educational Researcher,* 1982, *11*(4), 4-9.

Tuma, D. T., and Reif, F. (Eds.). *Problem Solving and Education: Issues in Teaching and Research.* Hillsdale, N.J.: Erlbaum, 1980.

Webb, N. M. "Student Interaction and Learning in Small Groups." *Review of Educational Research,* 1982, *52*(3), 421-445.

Wolfgang, M. E., and Dowling, W. D. "Differences in Motivation of Adult and Younger Undergraduates." *Journal of Higher Education,* 1981, *52*(6), 640-648.

Zajonc, R. B. "Feeling and Thinking: Preferences Need No Inferences." *American Psychologist,* 1980, *35,* 151-172.

Zander, A. F. "The Discussion Period in a College Classroom." *Memo to the Faculty,* No. 62. Ann Arbor: Center for Research on Learning and Teaching, University of Michigan, 1979.

Index

36-37; self-esteem of, 157, 163-164; self-sustaining, 160-161

Teaching: center on, functions of, 143-148; for concept comprehension, 69-82; conclusion on, 164-165; consistency in, 16, 138-139; and course content, 13-26; to enhance long-term memory, 57-60; evaluation of, 127-140; functions of, 37-38; of independent thinking, 83-96; institutional support for, 141-151; as interactive process, 5; lasting measure of, 1-11; learning connected with, 4-6; by lecturing, 28-31; many measures of, 2-6; and meaning, memory, and motivation measures, 6-11; methods of, and course content, 21-22; and motivation, 41-51; and options for presenting information, 27-39; remote measures of, 2-4; requirements for, 8-9; research interrelated with, 158-159; science of, 84-87; strength in, 9-10; substance and style in, 10-11; sunburn theory of, 15; sustaining good, 153-165; technological aids to, 31-34

Technological aids: book as, 31-33; computers as, 34-37; future of, 37-39; institutional support for, 146-147; lessons from, 37; visual image as, 33-34

Term papers, evaluation of, 120-121

Tests and testing: appraisal of results of, 114-115; for concept comprehension, 81-82; essay form of, 119-120; instructional use of, 113-115; and memory, 60; objective form of, 117-119; study skills for, 105-106; teacher-made forms of, 116-121

Thinking. *See* Independent thinking and learning

Thorndike, E. L., 44

Thune, L. E., 74, 174

Tobias, S., 85, 174

Tuma, D. T., 95, 174

V

Validity: of objective tests, 117; of student ratings for teachers, 134-135

Value judgments: and course content, 22-23; and lectures, 30; as teaching function, 38

Visual image, information from, 33-34

W

Ware, J. E., 29, 172

Webb, N. M., 65, 174

Wolfgang, M. E., 106, 174

Wright, C. R., 4, 171

Writing, study skills for, 104-105

Z

Zajonc, R. B., 50, 174

Zander, A. F., 65, 174